MY BODY BROKEN

MY BODY BROKEN

by

MELVIN A. HAMMARBERG

A Book for Lent

FORTRESS PRESS
PHILADELPHIA • ROCK ISLAND

MY BODY BROKEN

© *1963 by Fortress Press*

Library of Congress Catalog Card Number 62-20740

PRINTED
IN U S A

To all the families on earth who by their
prayers daily entertain the Christ,
especially to my own family,
this book is inscribed.

Introduction

The season of Lent directs the "eyes of faith" to the center of Christian truth, the passion of our Lord — his suffering, crucifixion on the cross, death on Good Friday, and resurrection on Easter. It is a penitential time, an intensive Christian training period in the Church Year. Dr. Eugene R. Fairweather has written, "Lent should be an atmosphere that surrounds us, an experience that gets into our flesh and nerves and bones, a way of life."[1] Few fields of Christian literature are so rich in resource material as that dealing with the passion of our Lord. That this holy season may find Christ's life touching and penetrating our lives is a necessary prayer of all of us.

How can we best use this holy season? How can we involve ourselves more deeply in the meaning and message of Lent? How can the life in Christ come more completely and fully into our lives? These are questions which the message of the church attempts to answer, even though the answers may be incomplete and imperfect.

Interest today in prayer is deep and world wide. The multiplication of requests for prayer, the increasing formation of prayer organizations, and many other stirrings indicate that among Christians everywhere there is an earnest desire to engage more fully in the privilege of intercession. Prayer is an expression of faith, and failure here is a loss in the inner and dynamic character of fellowship with the Eternal. In prayer, the living God actually deals with any man. Our Lord did not say, "If you pray;" instead He said, "When you pray." There come times in any life when there is need to tell the heavenly Father what is in the heart. "And whatever you ask in prayer, you will receive, if you have faith."[a] The privilege of prayer can be an inspiration and a help to men everywhere.

The Lenten Season can be a time for the reading of books about Christian faith and life. In this twentieth century when a mass of casual, superficial, and sometimes soiled literature pours constantly at people, it is good discipline to assume the reading of serious, substantial literature. Select a book having to do with Christian doctrine or practice. Resolve to let Lent be a time for concentrating on worth-while literary material. Also, it is appropriate in this vein to emphasize strongly the Book of Books, so that our reading includes the book central to Christendom, the Holy Bible. The reading of God's Word can become a tonic to any life, putting the vitamins of truth into daily living.

Lent is linking to the solemn and joyful announcement of the "good news." The birth and life, the death and resurrection, of Jesus Christ are at the heart of Christianity, and Lent is the invitation to all men grasped by these events to grow and participate in them. It invites Christians to prepare themselves for the celebration of the fulfilling festival of Christendom — Easter — and this preparation will involve penitence and discipline. Lent means examination under the Holy Spirit. It insists on the need for repentance and confession. It repeatedly announces a great forgiveness available to all in the broken body of Jesus. It has to do with real life for real people in their relationships with the living God.

To help all of us become more completely involved in the meaning of this season, its pilgrimage of prayer, its substantial literature, and its rigorous discipline, a central theme for this book has been selected. The title is "My Body Broken."

The first converts to Christianity "devoted themselves to the apostles' teaching and fellowship, to the breaking of bread and the prayers."[b] All accounts of early and later Christian

---

[a] Matt. 21:22
[b] Acts 2:42

life make it plain that these great emphases were followed as faith spread and the community grew. Again, in this year of our Lord, each of us is invited to commit himself to a life of faith and obedience in the presence of our crucified and risen Lord. Here the family of God advances step by step toward the gate of life, which his death and resurrection have opened to all. Again and anew, the invitation is extended, "This is my body broken" for you.

MELVIN A. HAMMARBERG

Contents

THINK UPON THE CROSS

I sometimes think upon the Cross
  And close my eyes, and try to see
The cruel nails—the crown of thorns,
  And Jesus crucified for me.

But even could I see him die,
  I could but see a little part
Of that eternal love, which like a fire
  Is always burning in his heart.

ANONYMOUS

PRAYER OF THE PASSION OF OUR LORD

O Lord Jesus Christ, Son of the Living God, who for our redemption, was willing to be born, — circumcised, — reprobated by the Jews,—delivered up by Judas' kiss,—taken and bound,—and carried in chains before Annas, Caiaphas, Herod, and Pilate, — mocked before them, — struck in the face, — smitten with scourge and reed, — to have thy face veiled and spit upon, — crowned with thorns, — accused by false witnesses, — judged, — and as an innocent Lamb, bearing thy Cross, led forth for sacrifice, — pierced with nails, — given gall and vinegar to drink, — and condemned to the most infamous death on the Cross, — and to be wounded with the lance: Do thou, by these most sacred expiations, free us from all sins and punishment, and through thy holy Cross bring us miserable sinners where thou didst lead the thief, crucified with thee, on his late repentance, to be with thyself eternally; who livest and reignest with the Father and the Holy Ghost, One God, world without end. Amen.[2]

Christ hath humbled himself and become obedient unto death, even the death of the Cross.

The Scripture

"And when you fast, do not look dismal, like the hypocrites, for they disfigure their faces that their fasting may be seen by men. Truly, I say to you, they have their reward. But when you fast, anoint your head and wash your face, that your fasting may not be seen by men but by your Father who is in secret; and your Father who sees in secret will reward you. Do not lay up for yourselves treasures on earth, where moth and rust consume and where thieves break in and steal, but lay up for yourselves treasures in heaven, where neither moth nor rust consumes and where thieves do not break in and steal. For where your treasure is, there will your heart be also."

Matthew 6: 16-21

THE PRAYER FOR THE DAY

Almighty God, Father everlasting, be near to us in this Lenten season of meditation and communion. May our hearts be open to every affection, and ready to receive and cherish every sacred memory and serious impression. Give us to know the power of that life and death which the season commemorates. Let a portion of the Spirit which led our Savior to the cross descend upon us and fill our hearts with love to God and man. Here and now may every selfish passion and desire be stilled and may the peace of God which passeth all understanding keep our hearts and minds in Christ Jesus, our Lord. Amen.[3]

Ash Wednesday is the first day in Lent. This strange name comes from an old Christian tradition in which penitent people clothed themselves in sackcloth and placed ashes on their heads after completing their prayers. Sometimes the ashes were made from the palm branches used on the previous Palm Sunday. The sackcloth and ashes were outward symbols of inner contrition, and great stress was placed on the need for the inner spirit of repentance. This tradition out of the past has been carried into the present day, so that Ash Wednesday marks the beginning of a season when the church invites Christians to practice self-denial and to seek inner renewal.

Where does life find renewal? It is not downstream in the broad flatlands and levees of plans and structures and techniques. It is rather far upstream in those solitary conversations when any man faces the mighty acts of God being carried on quietly, redemptively, by the outpouring of his living Spirit.

The writer, Carl G. Jung, wrote these weighty words, "We have built a monumental world about us, and we have slaved for it with unequalled energy. But it is so imposing because we have spent upon the outside all that is imposing in our natures; and what we find when we look within must necessarily be as it is, shabby and insufficient."[4] How many of us would willingly flee to that inwardness, which will renew the enfeebled and impoverished life of the Spirit? Renewing interior life is what the Lenten season is all about, and the great message of it is invitation to communion with Christ, whose body is broken and whose blood is shed, so that he can speak to us in that hidden chamber of the human heart. Here he can say to us that it is about time that his life become our own, for he has taken our lives as his own.

THE LORD'S PRAYER

Material favors draw us away from Christ, but the Cross always draws us to him. And God does not want the world to have us! He wants us for himself because he died for us.

The Scripture

"I will follow you wherever you go." And Jesus Christ said to him, "Foxes have holes, and birds of the air have nests; but the Son of man has nowhere to lay his head." To another he said, "Follow me." But he said, "Lord, let me first go and bury my father." But he said to him, "Leave the dead to bury their own dead; but as for you, go and proclaim the kingdom of God." Another said, "I will follow you, Lord; but let me first say farewell to those at my home." Jesus said to him, "No one who puts his hand to the plow and looks back is fit for the kingdom of God." Luke 9: 57b-62

THE PRAYER FOR THE DAY

Dear Savior, open our eyes to see that our forgetfulness of thee is the beginning of ruin. Give us light to see, O Lord, that it was sin which hardened itself into thy nails, wove itself into thy thorns, and congealed itself into thy Cross.

Let us also see that if thou didst take the cross for us, then we must be worth saving. If the crucifixion is the measure of our sinfulness, then the Cross is the pledge of our redemption. Help us hear the call in that Cross to follow thee day by day. Amen.

The call of Christ is in his cross, and his cross is in the call. The Christian life is costly to anyone who follows the Crucified. Jesus invites no one to follow him under false pretenses. His invitation makes very plain the high demands of his life. The Scripture for this day indicates three statements of advice to those who listen to his voice.

In reality he says, "If you want to follow me, count the cost." To be a Christian makes all the difference in the world, for it means giving total loyalty and allegiance to him and to no one and nothing else.

Jesus speaks to the second man in the lesson and reminds him that in life there is the matter of timing. When the proper moment is missed, it is unlikely that it will return. Jesus said that nothing, not even the matter of burial, should stand in the way of his invitation. Procrastination is a very human temptation. It is Jesus' insistence that when he calls we should hear. "Behold, now is the acceptable time; behold, now is the day of salvation."[a]

The third statement about Christian living is obvious. You cannot plow a straight furrow by looking back over your shoulder. Some people go into the future backward, with their hearts rooted in the past, forever thinking wistfully about "the good old days." An old man once said, "I hope you never suffer from a sunset." The Christian life has its gaze fixed on tomorrow, for it looks and longs for the dawn of a new day. Jesus' call is "Follow me forward!"

THE LORD'S PRAYER

---

[a] 2 Cor. 6:2b

A saint is a person who has quit worrying about himself, because his life is centered in God. Though his head and his hand be at labor, his heart dwells in the eternal.

The Scripture

"Beware of practicing your piety before men in order to be seen by them; for then you will have no reward from your Father who is in heaven.

"Thus, when you give alms, sound no trumpet before you, as the hypocrites do in the synagogues and in the streets, that they may be praised by men. Truly, I say to you, they have their reward. But when you give alms, do not let your left hand know what your right hand is doing, so that your alms may be in secret; and your Father who sees in secret will reward you.

"And when you pray, you must not be like the hypocrites; for they love to stand and pray in the synagogues and at the street corners, that they may be seen by men. Truly, I say to you, they have their reward. But when you pray, go into your room and shut the door and pray to your Father who is in secret; and your Father who sees in secret will reward you.

Matt. 6:1-6

THE PRAYER FOR THE DAY

All hail, dear Lord! Blessing and honor and glory and power be to thee. Root out, we pray thee, every wrong motive from our hearts. Pardon us, O Redeemer, for having preferred temporary rewards and perishing things to thee. Give us patience, humility, self-control and, above all, trust in thy mercy. Help us neither to rejoice in riches, if we have them, nor to covet them, if we lack them, but to practice generosity toward all people. Take from us hypocrisy, and give us the faith to accept the true riches of thy life. Shelter us under the shadow of thy love so that we may grow into thy likeness. Through Jesus Christ, our Lord. Amen.

6

Years ago a minister was on his way to a concert, when he passed a carriage stuck in the mud. Stopping his horse and buggy, he assisted the bemired man in continuing his travel and then was late for the musical. When he explained his delay, he was told, "You have missed all the singing." To which the pastor replied, "Yes, but I have songs in my heart." He received satisfaction from having done the Christlike act.

There are many motives for giving. One may give, not because he wishes to do so, but because he feels that giving is a duty he cannot escape. This kind of giving does not include any part of the giver and is thus incomplete. As James Russell Lowell puts it, "The gift without the giver is bare." Or a man may give for reasons of prestige, expecting and desiring thanks and praise and honor for what has been done. His giving is not to the glory of God but to the glory of himself.

The perfect example of giving is Jesus Christ himself. We give to others as Jesus Christ gave himself to us. Giving must be the overflow of the loved and loving heart.

If you pray in such a way as to parade your piety in the face of men, you may gain the reputation of being a saintly person, but that becomes your payment in full. Real prayer is an offering to God. When Jesus prayed, he met somebody. His life was linked to another life. He sensed a presence that disturbed him to the joy of higher things. Prayer is not begging for things nor is it self-communion. It is the loftiest experience within life — communion with God. The great gift of God in prayer is himself.

THE LORD'S PRAYER

Be present, O Lord, through the many hours of life, so that wearied by work or by the changes of this tempestuous world, we may rest our lives in the unchangeableness of Jesus Christ, our Lord.

The Scripture

Immediately he made his disciples get into the boat and go before him to the other side, to Bethsaida, while he dismissed the crowd. And after he had taken leave of them, he went into the hills to pray. And when evening came, the boat was out on the sea, and he was alone on the land. And he saw that they were distressed in rowing, for the wind was against them. And about the fourth watch of the night he came to them, walking on the sea. He meant to pass by them, but when they saw him walking on the sea they thought it was a ghost, and cried out; for they all saw him, and were terrified. But immediately he spoke to them and said, "Take heart, for it is I; have no fear." And he got into the boat with them and the wind ceased. And they were utterly astounded, for they did not understand about the loaves, but their hearts were hardened.　　Mark 6:45-52

THE PRAYER FOR THE DAY

O thou loving Father of us all, who art here and everywhere, whose power and peace have touched our lives in their deepest hours of distress, accept our thanks for thy great support in our time of need. Keep us confident and cheerful, give us patience and courage, so that we may turn to life's demands with a sense of stability and strength given by thee. Help us to find thy will in our lives as we follow thee from day to day. Be with those who wake or watch or weep this day and give thine angels charge concerning them. Be thou the strength of those who turn to thee, and give newness of life and peace to all who are tempest tossed. Through success and failure, victory and defeat, life and death, assure us of thy presence. In the name of him, who called us to himself. Amen

Jesus often used silence and solitude for conversation with God in prayer. This was his regular practice. He used prayer not as a form but as a force. Scripture relates that many times Jesus prayed with such joy that the fashion of his face was changed with the glory of it. He assumed that prayer would be a normal and natural part of life. Like Jesus, all of us need prayer for guidance and to keep holy conversation with God as we make our journey toward eternity.

After praying, Jesus looked up and saw the boat on the Sea of Galilee with his men in it having a difficult time to reach the other side because of a storm. Seeing their difficulty, Jesus turned from prayer and gave his attention to them, for there come times when praying must be replaced by action. Jesus, forgetting himself, went quickly to the help of his friends, for the cry of human need superseded all other claims upon him.

What happened is not written and cannot be known except that when he came into the storm, the sea became calm. St. Augustine has commented about this experience in these words, "He came treading the waves, and so he puts all the wild tumults of life under his feet. Christians need not be afraid." The experience of men and women in every generation reaffirms that when Christ is present any storm becomes a calm, the tempest becomes peace, and men are permitted to live like heroes through the impossible. The unexpected resources of Jesus can give any life staying power. To walk with Christ is to conquer with courage life's challenges and change.

THE LORD'S PRAYER

O Jesus, King most wonderful,
    Thou Conqueror renowned,
Thou sweetness most ineffable,
    In whom all joys are found!

When once thou visitest the heart,
    Then truth begins to shine,
Then earthly vanities depart,
    Then kindles love divine.

O Jesus, light of all below,
    Thou fount of life and fire,
Surpassing all the joys we know,
    All that we can desire;

May every heart confess thy Name,
    And ever thee adore,
And, seeking thee, itself inflame
    To seek thee more and more.

Thee may our tongues forever bless;
    Thee may we love alone,
And ever in our lives express
    The image of thine own.

Ascribed to St. Bernard of Clairvaux, 1091-1153
Tr. Edward Caswall, 1814-1878

LIVE WITH THE LIFT OF HIS LIFE

The Scripture

> Therefore God has highly exalted him and bestowed on
> him the name which is above every name, that at the name
> of Jesus every knee should bow, in heaven and on earth
> and under the earth, and every tongue confess that Jesus
> Christ is Lord, to the glory of God the Father.
>
> Philippians 2:9-11

He built no temple, yet the farthest sea
Can yield no shore that's barren of his place
For bended knee.
He wrote no book, and yet his words and prayer
Are intimate on many myriad tongues,
Are counsel everywhere.
The life he lived has never been assailed,
Nor any precept, as he lived it, yet
Has ever failed.
He built no kingdom, yet a king from youth
He reigned, is reigning yet; they call his realm
The Kingdom of the Truth.[5]

One figure has split all of time in two! Since he has come
everything is either before or after his advent. He is the
watershed of human history. Influential, powerful, extraordinary, he stands unique and incomparable as the greatest
man who has ever lived, even though for many he is a man
nobody knows.

Who is Jesus Christ? Is he an outstanding figure in
history? Is he a revered and remembered person? Or is
he a persuasive living presence?

The Gospel by Matthew announces that redemption
comes in him, after centuries of anticipation and Messianic
dreams. The Gospel of Mark speaks of him as the restless
Christ, ever seeking men that they in turn may discover
him. The Gospel by Luke tells of his healing touch in

11

the lives of men and identifies him as the Great Physician. The Gospel by John reveals Christ's relationship with the inner life of man, and identifies him with the hopes, aspirations, secrets, and prayers of people. A composite picture of Jesus is best given in this Scripture, "And there is salvation in no one else, for there is no other name under heaven given among men by which we must be saved."[a]

A Christian acclaims that the highest and best in life comes when Christ comes! He puts energy and purpose into living, so that every virtue possessed, every victory achieved, and every thought of holiness gained is a gift from him. Acquaintance with Jesus Christ is the very secret of life itself. John once wrote like this, "And this is eternal life, that they know thee the only true God, and Jesus Christ whom thou hast sent."[b]

We may see him first as a historical person. To read history is to reckon with him, for his footprints have imprinted the pathways of time. It must be acknowledged that he was there, a present power in the lives of men, and a dynamic force in all the ages since his coming. If we have learned this, great indeed is our discovery, for he is there in the centuries, a more significant person than any other.

Had he been reared as royalty, had he found fortune, had he comanded the military, then history might explain his influence to us and his prominence and place. But he was born in a manger; he had no wealth nor financial worth, and he directed no army. He had no power in this world except the naked power of his divine manhood.

James D. Francis has described him like this: "Here is a man who was born in an obscure village, the child of a peasant woman. He grew up in another obscure vil-

---

[a] Acts 4:12
[b] John 17:3

12

lage. He worked in a carpenter shop until he was thirty, and then for three years he was an itinerant preacher. He never wrote a book. He never held an office. He never owned a home. He never had a family. He never went to college. He never put his foot inside a big city. He never traveled two hundred miles from the place where he was born. He never did one of the things that usually accompany greatness. He had no credentials but himself.

". . . While still a young man, the tide of popular opinion turned against him. His friends ran away. One of them denied him. He was turned over to his enemies. He went through the mockery of a trial. He was nailed to a cross between two thieves. His executioners gambled for the only piece of property he had on earth, while he was dying— and that was his coat. When he was dead, he was taken down and laid in a borrowed grave through the pity of a friend.

"Nineteen wide centuries have come and gone, and today he is the centerpiece of the human race and the leader of the column of progress.

"I am far within the mark when I say that all the armies that ever marched, and all the navies that ever were built, and all the parliaments that ever sat, and all the kings that ever reigned, put together, have not affected the life of man upon this earth as powerfully as has that One Solitary Life."

Who is Jesus? "I believe that Jesus Christ is true man," states the Catechism. Scripture often acknowledges him with the name, "the Son of Man." When the disciples met Jesus they recognized him first of all as a man. He played with little children, laughed with his friends and was fond of people. Once he was called a "wine bibber." In all his social relations he had a common touch. In three years, he did in love what no other has been able to do. He lived a life of peace and power. He was a man without divided loyalties, selfish inter-

13

ests, or fears. He worked ceaselessly and carefully in serving others and in lifting all of life.

Society has many kinds of people. There are those who do evil deliberately like Shylock in "The Merchant of Venice" or Judas among the Twelve. These people contribute nothing but wrong into the river of life. Then there are individuals who try to do good and are like most people. When evil appears in their lives, it is error and trespass. For in people there is something of deity and dirt, mystery and meanness. How men need understanding for others and the forgiving mercy of Almighty God! And then there is Jesus, the Son of Man, who towers radiant above the gloom, living a life free from sin which makes people despicable to themselves and to others. When he came as a man he brought a new warmth and a new light into life like the morning sun dispelling the mists and shadows of night.

Jesus seemed so fragile over against the power of the world, amidst the grasping greed of men, and surrounded by the struggle of nations. But he continued to be a friend to the forlorn, to speak good tidings to the hopeless, and to bring to men two significant salutations, "Be of good cheer," and "Be not afraid." He was the Son of man who lived for others!

Who is Jesus? "I believe that Jesus Christ . . . is my Lord." He is the Savior. "You shall call his name Jesus, for he will save his people from their sins."ᶜ As Savior, Jesus saves man from himself, from his sin, and from death.

Today man looks with pride on his own works. Yet he is confused and confounded. There are so many loyalties bidding for the allegiance of his mind and heart. His life is like a television set that has caught two channels simultaneously with nothing more resulting than an oblong blur. He is like a man trying to drive in all directions at the same time, only to discover that it cannot be done. A baggage sign in Hong Kong

---
ᶜ Matt. 1.21

14

reads, "Your baggage delivered in all directions." Man's life much of the time is like this baggage service — going in all directions. There is such a disparity between what he ought to do and what he does do, that his world is split into many worlds — body, eyes, mind, spirit. The poet put it this way:

Within my earthly temple there's a crowd;
There's one of us that's humble, one that's proud,
There's one broken-hearted for his sins,
There's one that unrepentant sits and grins;
There's one that loves his neighbor as himself
And one that cares for naught but fame and self.
From much corroding care I should be free,
If I could once determine which is me.[6]

Man is sinful and begins to acknowledge his wickedness. The evil in society is simply the sum total and piling up of the kind of sin that lives and lurks in any life. Yet, how often human behavior is rationalized. A psychological explanation says, "I am what I am because when reading a murder mystery during a thunder storm, I was frightened by a mouse."

The explanation of education reads like this, "If we had more schools and more education, we would be better people." But education may be only the difference between being an ignorant devil or an educated one. The discoveries of science may simply mean that evil can travel farther and faster.

The rationalization of wealth says, "If I had more money, I would be a better person." However, a gold bit does not make a better horse, though it might become more attractive.

Man is mortal, and must acknowledge his mortality. The obituary column in every newspaper and the cemeteries in every community are silent symbols of transiency. Life is hung by a thread. It walks on eggshells. One day life is here, the next day it is in the hereafter.

Into this setting Jesus Christ comes as the Savior of men. He pulls life together and gives it unity, coherence, and wholeness. Just as a burning glass pulls together the rays of the sun and brings them into focus with burning power, so the Savior gathers together the scattered, broken fragmentation of life and transforms it into oneness; giving it unity, cohesiveness, and a center. Jesus Christ gives life focus and grants the gifts of poise and purpose. The Apostle Paul once wrote, "By him all things consist."[d] A modern translator has written it even more plainly, "All things are held together in him."[e]

Jesus Christ, as Savior, forgives human sin. The explanation for human behavior, given by Scripture, is painfully accurate. "If we say we have no sin, we deceive ourselves."[f] Joad once wrote, "Sin is endemic in the human family." It flows in our veins; it resides in our human nature; it is a part of us. But Christ Jesus announces from the pulpit of the cross, "Father, forgive them,"[g] and again he said, "'Take heart, my son; your sins are forgiven.'"[h]

John Ruskin, in his book, *Modern Painters,* tells about the soil outside of a factory city. He says it has four component parts — clay, sand, soot, and water. With his keen creative imagination, Ruskin suggests that if the clay is pressed together with tremendous force and then held in the sunlight, it becomes an emerald. The sand, congealed in the same way, becomes a sparkling sapphire. The soot, crystalized and placed in the sun, becomes a diamond, and the water sprinkled on the grass before the morning sun, becomes nature's loveliest jewel, an exquisite dewdrop. In a much higher manner, God takes our lives with their impurities and imperfections, compresses them in the hard and narrow way of repentance, and holds them in the sunlight of one who is called the Son of

---

[d] Col. 1:17, KJV
[e] Col. 1:16, The New English Bible
[f] 1 John 1:8
[g] Luke 23:34
[h] Matt. 9:2

Righteousness, until we receive to ourselves a loveliness not of our making but of his.

Jesus Christ is the Savior from death. When the doctor has carefully closed his case; the nurse has quietly shut the door, and the eloquence of death is heard, he is the only one who has a word of hope to say beside the silent sod. By his resurrection from the tomb on an Easter day, he becomes the death of Death, and the Lord of Life.

Who is Jesus? "I believe that Jesus Christ . . . begotten of the Father from eternity" is the Son of God! Jesus Christ is a person, "for in him the whole fulness of deity dwells bodily."[i] According to the Scriptures, he was also "of the Holy Spirit."

The statements of Jesus about himself are astonishing and incredible. He deliberately places himself at the very heart of his gospel, and invites devotion to his own person. He equates himself with God. "He who has seen me has seen the Father,"[j] "I and the Father are one,"[k] and, "He who loves his life for my sake will find it,"[l] are the unprecedented claims that he made for himself. So strange that sayings like these on the lips of any other person would sound preposterous, but from Jesus they seem fitting and proper.

Listen to those who lived with Jesus, encountered him personally, and can testify most fully to who he really is.

Pilate, what do you think of this man? "I find no crime in this man."[m]

Judas, you who betrayed him for thirty pieces of silver, have you a charge to hurl? "I have sinned in betraying innocent blood."[n]

---

[i] Col. 2:9
[j] John 14:9
[k] John 10:30
[l] Matt. 10:39
[m] Luke 23:4
[n] Matt. 27:4

Centurion, you who nailed him to the Cross—what is your testimony? "Truly this man was a son of God!"[o]

Demons, you, who know his power — do you have a word? "You are the Son of God."[p]

John the Baptist, what is your witness? "Behold, the Lamb of God!"[q]

Peter, you who denied him three times — what do you say? "Thou art the Christ, . . ."[r]

Thomas, you were in doubt for a long while? What is your word? "My Lord and my God!"[s]

Paul, you persecuted him? What do you say? "I count everything as loss because of the surpassing worth of knowing Christ Jesus my Lord."[t]

Angels in heaven, what is your testimony? "For to you is born this day in the city of David a Savior, who is Christ the Lord."[u]

And heavenly Father, can your voice be heard? "This is my beloved Son, with whom I am well pleased."[v]

Jesus Christ is Lord, and his life was lived not only once in history long ago, but is a living presence today. His radiant humanity sheds its light upon the way we walk. His full salvation crowns our living with peace. His Lordship is life eternal!

As we study him in the Scriptures, he examines us in the light of his life. It is difficult to look at the crucifixion without sensing personal involvement. When we seek the Lord, we know that he has long sought us. We did not choose him; he chose us! Jesus Christ is Lord!

---

[o] Mark 15:39
[p] Mark 3:11
[q] John 1:36
[r] Matt. 16:16
[s] John 20:28
[t] Phil. 3:8
[u] Luke 2:11
[v] Matt. 17:5

18

Life's ultimate resolution is either to serve self or to glorify God. A world in which man's highest purpose is to serve self is a world of savagery, unending strife, and deep division.

The Scripture

What causes wars, and what causes fighting among you? Is it not your passions that are at war in your members? You desire and do not have; so you kill. And you covet and cannot obtain; so you fight and wage war. You do not have, because you do not ask. You ask and do not receive, because you ask wrongly, to spend it on your passions. Unfaithful creatures! Do you not know that friendship with the world is enmity with God? Therefore whoever wishes to be a friend of the world makes himself an enemy of God. Or do you suppose it is in vain that the scripture says, "He yearns jealously over the spirit which he has made to dwell in us?" But he gives more grace; therefore it says, "God opposes the proud, but gives grace to the humble." Submit yourselves therefore to God. Resist the devil and he will flee from you. Draw near to God and he will draw near to you.

James 4:1-8

THE PRAYER FOR THE DAY

If from all thy good gifts, O Lord, I may ask but one, let that one be the spirit of kindness!

Let others have fame and fortune and jewels and palaces, if I may but have the kindly spirit! Give greatness and power to those that want them, but give to me Brotherly Kindness! Make somebody else to be comely of visage, if only I may wear a kindly countenance.

May I never wound the heart of any faltering child of thine! Make me to do the little unremembered acts that quietly help without intending it. Grant me to bear about the unconscious radiance of a life that knows no grudge, but loves all men because they are children of my Father who loved them enough to send his Son to save them. Amen.[31]

GEORGE A. MILLER

20

"Tension" is a word that has received a prominent place in our vocabulary during the past ten years. International tension, interracial tension and interreligious tension are three catalogs of this modern stress and strain in the world's life Another analysis lists the struggles between the old and the new, between the individual and the group, and between the dignity of personality and the insatiable quest for economic betterment. What is the cause of some of these strained human relationships?

The writer, James, indicates that basic causes for unwholesome tension in today's world are to be found in the selfishness of the human heart, the desire for possessions and power, and in the lusts of life. The spirit of today teaches us to lay up for ourselves as much as we can according to human fancy, but the Spirit of God teaches us to do good to all about us as we are able. Divorced from God, man is proud and seeks pleasure. He entertains lust and seeks satisfaction. He struggles in war and seeks to conquer. Even prayer is sometimes employed, James suggests, for these unworthy goals.

Christian living means to submit human understanding to the truth of God, human impulses to the will of God, and the human heart to the love of God. Sin in any of its dimensions should invite repentance and godly sorrow, for the Lord will not refuse to comfort one who really mourns for sin or to exalt anyone who is willing to practice the humility of faith.

THE LORD'S PRAYER

> *Life must have a center that will pull it together, give it a pattern and grant it peace. Such a focal point is the cross of Christ.*

The Scripture

Let no one say when he is tempted, "I am tempted by God": for God cannot be tempted with evil and he himself tempts no one; but each person is tempted when he is lured and enticed by his own desire. Then desire when it has conceived gives birth to sin; and sin when it is full-grown brings forth death.

Do not be deceived, my beloved brethren. Every good endowment and every perfect gift is from above, coming down from the Father of lights with whom there is no variation or shadow due to change. Of his own will he brought us forth by the word of truth that we should be a kind of first fruits of his creatures. — **James 1: 13-18**

THE PRAYER FOR THE DAY

O Lord Jesus Christ, who in the wilderness didst know the loneliness of temptation; give us grace and courage to stand with thee when others tempt us to betray thee. Save us from a false sense of superiority when we mingle with those who do not strive in all things to follow thee. Help us to move among them with patience, sympathy, and good will. Put thy light in our hearts and show us the reasons of righteousness. Grant us the joy of clean living and help us to see beyond the passing pleasure to the larger good. Give us grace to be steadfast among evil companions and be thou ever our unseen companion and our Lord. Amen.

It is easy to rationalize undesirable human behavior and to evade personal responsibility for it by blaming others. When Adam was faced with his disobedience in the Garden of Eden, he quickly blamed Eve by saying, "The woman whom thou gavest to be with me, she gave me fruit of the tree, and I ate."[a] When Eve, in turn, was challenged, she placed the blame on the serpent. Often man says that his villainous deportment is determined by his companions, by circumstances, or by creation, and so easily relieves himself of any responsibility. Even God is blamed for human wickedness.

However, would not sin be helpless, if there were no harboring of it in the human heart? If temptation to evil received no response, how could it be nourished or sustained? Is not every man ultimately responsible for his personal conduct? Before evil becomes an act, it is thought in the mind, and before it becomes a part of the intellect, it is temptation to badness. Mind and heart and eyes and feet and lips can be used to entertain wickedness.

Satan is the tempter who flings around life that which drags down and creates dullness and death of spirit. Resistance to wrong reinforces character and leads to that strength out of which the stuff of life is made. It is God alone, through Jesus Christ, who leads us through temptation into that power where evil is not entertained nor easy, and the good gifts of grace are accepted to become life abundant. The Apostle Paul writes, "Finally, brethren, whatever is true, whatever is honorable, whatever is just, whatever is pure, whatever is lovely, whatever is gracious, if there is any excellence, if there is anything worthy of praise, think about these things."[b]

THE LORD'S PRAYER

---

[a] Gen. 3:12
[b] Phil. 4:8

Faith reaches up to the God, who has reached down in his Son to hold the years and the spheres in his hands.

The Scripture

Since then we have a great high priest who has passed through the heavens, Jesus, the Son of God, let us hold fast our confession. For we have not a high priest who is unable to sympathize with our weaknesses, but one who in every respect has been tempted as we are, yet without sinning. Let us then with confidence draw near to the throne of grace, that we may receive mercy and find grace to help in time of need.   Hebrews 4: 14-16

The Prayer for the Day

Ah, Lord God, Thou holy lover of my soul, when thou comest into my soul, all that is within me shall rejoice. Thou art my glory and the exultation of my heart; thou art my hope and refuge in the day of my trouble. Set me free from all evil passions, and heal my heart of all inordinate affections; that, being inwardly cured and thoroughly cleansed, I may be made fit to love, courageous to suffer, steady to persevere. Nothing is sweeter than love, nothing more courageous, nothing fuller nor better in heaven and earth; because love is born of God, and cannot rest but in God, above all created things. Let me love thee more than myself, nor love myself but for thee. Amen.

THOMAS á KEMPIS

Much of life anywhere can be routine and monotonous until Jesus Christ comes and transforms everything into newness. He brings freshness into the common round of any day. He is a permeator of life and not a separator from it, always improving the quality of living. Christ is not one who is indifferent to, unacquainted with, or unaware of, our human circumstance. His life was touched and clothed with our humanity.

He experienced temptation as we do, yet remained free from sin. His temptations had a threefold appeal, to the lust of the flesh, the lure of the eyes, and the pride of life. In the wilderness, his temptation was first to make stones into bread, which became an appeal to bodily desire. Then he was shown all the kingdoms of the world, which was an appeal to the lure of the eyes, and finally in the suggestion that he cast himself from the pinnacle of the temple in order to become ruler, there came the appeal to the pride of life. In each of these instances the temptation to evil was overcome by the power of God's Word.

As enthroned Savior and conqueror, He is now interceding for us, and the invitation is universal and free for all to come to the Source of mercy, and to receive grace adequate for life's demands. Christ becomes the comfort of the lonely, the forgiveness for every sin, and the crown of life. He lives as Savior and Sovereign forever!

THE LORD'S PRAYER

*Irenaeus said years ago, "No prophecy is fully under-
stood until after the fulfillment of it."*

The Scripture

The Passover of the Jews was at hand, and Jesus went up to
Jerusalem. In the temple he found those who were selling oxen
and sheep and pigeons, and the money-changers at their business. And making a whip of cords, he drove them all, with the
sheep and oxen, out of the temple; and he poured out the
coins of the money-changers and overturned their tables. And
he told those who sold the pigeons, "Take these things away;
you shall not make my Father's house a house of trade." His
disciples remembered that it was written, "Zeal for thy house
will consume me." The Jews then said to him, "What sign have
you to show us for doing this?" Jesus answered them, "Destroy
this temple, and in three days I will raise it up." The Jews
then said, "It has taken forty-six years to build this temple,
and you will raise it up in three days?" But he spoke of the
temple of his body. When therefore he was raised from the
dead, his disciples remembered that he had said this; and they
believed the scripture and the word which Jesus had spoken.

John 2: 13-22

THE PRAYER FOR THE DAY

*O God, I pray for thy church, which is set today amid the
perplexities of a changing order and face to face with a great
new task. I remember with love the nurture she gave to my
spiritual life in its infancy, the tasks she set for my growing
strength, the influence of the devoted hearts she gathers, the
steadfast power for good she has exerted. When I compare
her with all human institutions, there is none like her. But
when judged by the mind of her Master, I bow in contrition.
O God, baptise her afresh in the life-giving spirit of Jesus!
Put upon her lips the ancient gospel of her Lord. Fill her
with the prophet's scorn of tyranny, and with a Christlike
tenderness for the heavy-laden and downtrodden. Bid her cease
from seeking her own life, lest she lose it. Make her valiant
to give up her life to humanity, that like her crucified Lord
she may mount by the path of the Cross to a higher glory.
Amen.*

WALTER RAUSCHENBUSCH

The anger of Jesus is an awesome thing! The picture of Christ with a whip is a frightful sight. There must have been good reason for the display of anger on the part of the Master. The open extortion practiced in the Temple of that day at Passover time, at the expense of poor and humble pilgrims, was a glaring social injustice. It was even more reprehensible because it was practiced in the name of religion. Since he loved all people, it was impossible to be passive in the face of this kind of injustice. The cleansing of the Temple was accomplished by the Master because it was being desecrated by evil practices. Worship and reverence, realizing the holiness of the presence of God, were to be characteristics of the Temple. Arguments about prices, disputes about money, and the clatter and clutter of bargaining, were not appropriate to the spirit of worship in the Temple.

A church is a place for prayer. Undoubtedly Jesus was moved to the depths of his being because men seeking God were being distracted from a sense of his presence. Any church may well ask itself if there is that which distracts from its essential purpose, that of worshipping God in the name of the Master and of serving people.

But even in the cleansing of the Temple, Jesus is conscious of the stalking shadow of his coming crucifixion, burial and resurrection, for He said, "Destroy this temple, and in three days I will raise it up."[a]

THE LORD'S PRAYER

---

[a] John 2:19

27

SECOND FRIDAY IN LENT

> *Christian service brings sunshine to the paths of others, satisfaction to oneself, and a smile on the face of God.*

The Scripture

From that time Jesus began to show his disciples that he must go to Jerusalem and suffer many things from the elders and chief priests and scribes, and be killed, and on the third day be raised. And Peter took him and began to rebuke him, saying, "God forbid, Lord! This shall never happen to you." But he turned and said to Peter, "Get behind me, Satan! You are a hindrance to me; for you are not on the side of God, but of men."

Then Jesus told his disciples, "If any man would come after me, let him deny himself and take up his cross and follow me. For whoever would save his life will lose it, and whoever loses his life for my sake will find it. For what will it profit a man, if he gains the whole world and forfeits his life? Or what shall man give in return for his life? For the Son of Man is to come with his angels in the glory of his Father, and then he will repay every man for what he has done. Truly, I say to you, there are some standing here who will not taste death before they see the Son of man coming in his kingdom."

Matthew 16: 21-28

THE PRAYER FOR THE DAY

O God our Father, show us that we are thine, and that we cannot attain our real life until we give ourselves wholly to thee. Deliver us from self-service, and from the misery of a careless and halfhearted devotion, in which we are left to struggle in a never-ending war between our lower and our higher selves. Endue us with a passionate desire for a complete consecration, that our life in all its relations may be thine: make us little brothers of the Lord Jesus.

Accept our prayer, our Father; accomplish thy will in us. Teach us that the yearning within us is thy spirit, and that if we follow its light in thy face we shall see light. Help us to read the trials of life not as the accidents of earth, but as a divine discipline for the making of our souls. Grant us victory over dark moods and faithless fears, and bring us at last to the vision where faith and truth are blended; in Jesus Christ our Lord. Amen.

JOSEPH FORT NEWTON

Peter was so human. He was a man of impulse, full of impetuosity. He was quick "on the trigger." He suited his actions to the moment, moving first and thinking and reflecting later. He was no modest shrinking petunia. He was always foremost in talking and acting. It is no accident that his name is first in the listing of the Apostles.

It was difficult for Peter to imagine that Jesus was not to be king of power and glory and conquest, but rather a suffering Savior. The connection of the Messiah with the cross seemed incredible. It was this misunderstanding of the role of the Redeemer that evoked from Jesus the remark, "Get behind me, Satan!" The dominant characteristic of discipleship is surrender for service, for the Christian life involves self-denial. How difficult to say "No" to self and to say "Yes" to God!

The demands of Christian living involve keeping the right price tags on the right goods. Often the demands of duties, the discipline of faithfulness to serve people, and the willingness to "give not counting the cost," must take precedence over the comfort of the fireside, the pleasure of entertainment, or an inviting life of leisure. The Gospel by Luke adds the significant little word, "daily," to this theme by Jesus, as though to suggest that this life of redemptive cross-bearing is to be lived in a constant awareness of its demands. In a sense the Christian life is a follow-the-leader game, in which the Christian walks, as Charles M. Sheldon suggests, "in his steps." All of us owe everything we have and are to Jesus Christ, and the greatest possible gift that anyone can give in return is his whole life. No one can give more. Anything less will not do.

THE LORD'S PRAYER

In the fullness of time God lifted on time's horizon the sign of the Cross.

The Scripture

Then some of the scribes and Pharisees said to him, "Teacher, we wish to see a sign from you." But he answered them, "An evil and adulterous generation seeks for a sign; but no sign shall be given to it except the sign of the prophet Jonah. For as Jonah was three days and three nights in the belly of the whale, so will the Son of man be three days and three nights in the heart of the earth. The men of Nineveh will arise at the judgment with this generation and condemn it; for they repented at the preaching of Jonah, and behold, something greater than Jonah is here. The queen of the South will arise at the judgment with this generation and condemn it; for she came from the ends of the earth to hear the wisdom of Solomon, and behold, something greater than Solomon is here."

Matthew 12: 38-42

The Prayer for the Day

Grant me, even me, my dearest Lord, to know thee, and love thee, and rejoice in thee. And, if I cannot do these perfectly in this life, let me at least advance to higher degrees every day, till I can come to do them in perfection. Let the knowledge of thee increase in me here, that it may be full hereafter. Let the love of thee grow every day more and more here, that it may be perfect hereafter; that my joy may be great in itself, and full in thee. I know, O God, that thou art a God of truth; O make good thy gracious promises to me, that my joy may be full. Amen.

St. Augustine

ABOUT THE LESSON

Our present generation is often characterized as being pragmatic. We are tempted to say even in the realm of religion that only that which we can see and touch and taste is real. How often, childlike, we make the same request the disciples once made, "Lord, show us the Father."[a] If God would only step out of the trelliswork of the stars so that we could see him, faith would be easier.

Jesus is God's Son! Some may fail to recognize him, but he has come in his Word and in the sacraments as God's picture to us. He is more valid to our generation than was Jonah to his, and the wisdom he gives us is more plainly written than that of Solomon. In the matchless life of Jesus Christ we are confronted with God.

If Jesus is God's sign, then the Cross is his signature. His suffering and death are the collateral written in blood, that God's promises are sure and that his love is real. For even when men did to him the worst that they could do, he continued to be what love is, the complete giving of self. In the olden days men sometimes signed with an "X." God signed that way once, a Cross, his signature of grace fulfilled.

THE LORD'S PRAYER

---

[a] John 14:8

Jesus, thou Joy of loving hearts,
   Thou Fount of life, thou Light of men,
From the best bliss that earth imparts
   We turn unfilled to thee again.

Thy truth unchanged hath ever stood;
   Thou savest those that on thee call;
To them that seek thee thou art good,
   To them that find thee, all in all.

We taste thee, O thou living Bread,
   And long to feast upon thee still;
We drink of thee, the Fountainhead,
   And thirst our souls from thee to fill.

Our restless spirits yearn for thee,
   Where'er our changeful lot is cast;
Glad, when thy gracious smile we see,
   Blest, when our faith can hold thee fast.

O Jesus, ever with us stay;
   Make all our moments calm and bright;
Chase the dark night of sin away,
   Shed o'er the world thy holy light.

Ascribed to St. Bernard of Clairvaux, 1091-1153
Tr. Ray Palmer, 1808-87

HEAR THE WORDS OF HIS MOUTH

The Scripture

> "Man shall not live by bread alone, but by every word that
> proceeds from the mouth of God."   Matthew 4:4

Words are powerful! They sing. They sting. They hurt.
They heal. They keep man from the world of ignorance. They
are the basic means of human communication. A well-known
Chinese proverb states, "A picture is worth ten thousand
words." But a rapid reply reminds, "It takes words to say
that."

An author in a recent issue of *Look* magazine wrote, "We
live by words: love, truth, God. We fight for words: freedom,
country, fame. We die for words: liberty, glory, honor. They
bestow the priceless gift of articulacy on our minds and
hearts."[8]

Words are an index to a man's mind — "As the man, so his
speech." Listen to someone talk, and you can conclude that
the person is hard, cynical, and severe. Or listen to someone
else speak, and you are able to say, "He is kind, understanding, and sympathetic.

With his mouth, Jesus gave his message, and through the
words which he spoke, he has come to be known as the Incarnate Word of God to all mankind.

Jesus never wrote a book. On only one occasion is it reported that he wrote, and then it was on the shifting sand,
which the wind soon blew away, so that no man could any
longer read it. Though he had the greatest message of all to
give, yet he did not take the unusual precaution that would
have preserved it, and instead committed the words to the
ears and minds of his hearers. Jesus was a preacher not an
author. "For since, in the wisdom of God, the world did not

know God through wisdom, it pleased God through the folly of what we preach to save those who believe."[a]

People listened to his words. The multitudes followed him for "the common people heard him gladly." Once when soldiers tried to arrest him, they returned without their prisoner and gave as the strange reason for non-arrest, "No man ever spoke like this man."[b]

When men heard his words there was no forgetting them, for he spoke with precision, clarity, and grandeur. His words taught, inspired, and molded the destinies of people. They were engraved upon something more durable than paper or parchment, for they were written into the very lives of his hearers.

In his writing entitled, *The Book Nobody Knows,* Bruce Barton tells the story of a socially prominent lady, who was seated next to a bishop at a civic banquet. Knowing that most bishops enjoyed being met on common ground, when it came to conversation, she turned to the clergyman and said, "Do you know, bishop, the book I enjoy reading the most is the Bible." The bishop was surprised at this kind of conversation from this well-upholstered lady, and he replied, "What is it that you enjoy the most in the Bible?" Undaunted came the quick reply, "I like the passage which mentions the wind being tempered toward the shorn lamb." The bishop did not know the passage and suspected that it had as much relationship to the Bible as the Encyclopedia Britannica has to Robinson Crusoe, but he did not say so. "What passage in the Bible do you enjoy?" asked the lady. To which the bishop replied. "I like the passage which talks about Elijah crossing the Delaware."

Is it not true that most people know more about the center fielder for the Yankees than they know about the Apostle Paul? More about the leading actress on the screen than they

[a] 1 Cor. 1:21
[b] John 7:46

know about Miriam or Hannah? More about the news in to-day's newspaper than about the "good news" of God's Holy Word?

One of the liabilities of being born in America and being reared in a Christian home is that these living words of Jesus often become common, unnoticed, and unappreciated. Even the easy availability of these words cannot destroy their power nor rob them of their immortal beauty. The words of Jesus are as soft as velvet and as sturdy as oak. They are as timely as this moment's need and as timeless as the ages. Sometimes we say, "Talk is cheap." But that depends on who does the talking.

When a defendant stands before the bar of justice and the words "guilty" or "not guilty" are pronounced, the words are important because the liberty or imprisonment of the person is dependent upon them. When a couple stands at the altar and says, "I will," the words count because the future is involved in them. And so when we hear the words of Jesus, they are deeply significant because of the One who says them.

His Words Reveal. As Christ speaks he shows us ourselves and his Word becomes judgment. In the Book of Revelation by St. John we have a picture of the disturbing Christ: "From his mouth issued a sharp two-edged sword."[c] That was true of his words while he lived on earth, and it remains true of his words everlastingly. His words judge us as love judges hatred, as truth judges falsehood, and as goodness judges evil. The words that he uttered become a measuring rod for every man.

"The words that I have spoken to you," declared Jesus, "are spirit and life."[d] His words become a revelation of ourselves. The words of Jesus teach us much about human nature and human motives. Rich men, poor men, beggarmen, thieves — his words tell us that he knows all of them. The

[c] Rev. 1:16
[d] John 6:63

35

full spectrum of human behavior — love, hate, joy, jealousy — is known to him. He knows what is in man, and no one needs to tell him. Man reaches for righteousness but writhes in wretchedness. Man puffs himself up in pride and is punctured by failure. Man washes his hands of God but calls for him repeatedly. As Soren Kierkegaard suggests, his words become a mirror revealing man to himself. Jesus knows the heights to which man can soar, the nobleness that lives within him, and the hero in any human heart. But he also knows the depths of degradation to which man can fall and the iniquities, trespasses and sin, which so easily soil and stain human lives. The words of Jesus stalk all and his words haunt. "Unless you repent you will all likewise perish."[e]

The high and holy, discipline-demanding words of Jesus pursue relentlessly, pressing their claim for uprightness and decency, honesty and integrity in living. "Every one then who hears these words of mine," says Jesus, "will be like a wise man who built his house upon the rock."[f] The house of life built on the Rock of Ages will stand amidst the stress and strain, temptations and trials, of life. "But be doers of the word, and not hearers only."[g]

His Words Heal. By the words of his mouth, Jesus healed disease, soothed the mind of the mentally disturbed, and called the dead from their graves. Through his words, he pronounced for sinners the forgiveness of God. He removes forever in his mercy the burden of a guilty conscience and makes strong as ten the pure in heart. He inspires his followers to exclaim, "We are afflicted in every way, but not crushed; perplexed, but not driven to despair; persecuted, but not forsaken; struck down, but not destroyed."[h] To the bereaved and brokenhearted, He becomes the Master of Sorrows,

---

[e] Luke 13:3
[f] Matt. 7:24
[g] James 1:22
[h] 2 Cor. 4:8-9

helping those who mourn to see beyond the tears and the years. From his life came those stupendous claims which have shaken the world and transformed human life.

If your Christian biography reads anything like mine, it reads something like this. When I was a child, I attended church school and there learned the lessons and the truth of God. And later in life, when tempted to follow foolish and futile philosophies, the lessons and the life of Jesus became alive, inescapable and irresistible.

When I was a youth and knew the spirit of adventure and the optimism that characterizes any teen-ager, the church guided my steps by lifting my eyes to the stars of his Word.

When I fell deeply in love and then stood before the altar of the church, the words of Jesus, in hallowed benediction, spiritualized my affections and gave validity and strength to my marriage, so that the sun shone on a thousand hills.

Through the years, whenever my feet slipped, and I knew the bitterness of sin and acknowledged that there was in my life that for which heaven's mercy was needed, it was the healing words of Christ in the Sacrament of the Altar, which called me back to the heights of a better self and granted peace again.

When my life was seamed with sorrow and all hope was blotted out, it was then that the words of Jesus became my comfort and solace and put the stars of eternal hope back into my being.

The healing touch of his words is like the balm in Gilead and like a refrain from the psalmist of old, "Thy word is a lamp to my feet and a light to my path."[i]

His Words Appeal. Recall the Gospel by John, "In the beginning was the Word, and the Word was with God, and the Word was God. . . . And the Word became flesh and dwelt among us, full of grace and truth; we have beheld his glory,

---

[i] Psalm 119:105

37

glory as of the only Son from the Father."[j] Jesus Christ himself is the Word incarnate. He himself is the word of God — truth, light and love — demonstrated and lived in human form.

Consider what this means. If Jesus Christ is "the same yesterday and today and forever,"[k] then his words are free from mutation and fluctuation and become bedrock stability in a day of revolutionary change. All textbooks in institutions of learning become antiquated and out of date as human knowledge vacillates and changes, but the words of Jesus are changeless for this changing world and will survive the onrush of relentless time.

Christ is holy and his words are reflections of the beauty and excellence always ascribed to his name. His words are a complement to his flawless moral character and to the beauty of his grace. He was different from all sinners and from all saints in that he confessed to no sin for he had none, and his words echo this perfection. Lord Macaulay once said, "The words of Scripture alone suffice to show God's beauty and power."

Christ is truth. Legal truth so often involves a variety and disparity of information for it is seen through human eyes and spoken out of human minds. Scientific truth changes as the facts of research and academic inquiry continue to unfold and enlarge the storehouse of human knowledge. New Testament truth is the unveiling of the mystery in which our lives are held. Christ is this truth and his words as truth make men free.

Christ is love, all other loves excelling, and his language is altogether compassionate for the persecuted and oppressed, the least and the lost, the suffering and the sorrowful; but in its finality, his word is mercy to the sin-soiled lives of men. God forgives — the words of Jesus convey this forgiveness.

---

[j] John 1:1 and 14
[k] Heb. 13:8

38

God breaks the fetters of sin — the good news of grace through Jesus Christ snaps the chain. God redeems — the Word Incarnate is the Redeemer! Who can measure the wideness of the mercy of his words?

Christ is eternal! His matchless words are imperishable. Missiles and bombs, outer-space travel and inner-space travail, cannot shake or shatter the promise, "Heaven and earth shall pass away, but my words shall not pass away."[1]

He loves the world from the wood of the cross, and his words are a revelation of man, a therapy for life, and a compelling power for good.

Jesus said, "If you continue in my word, you are truly my disciples, and you will know the truth, and the truth will make you free."[m]

---

[1] Matt. 24:35
[m] John 8:31, 32

"What you are speaks so loudly, I cannot hear what you say."

The Scripture

About the middle of the feast Jesus went up into the temple and taught. The Jews marveled at it, saying, "How is it that this man has learning, when he has never studied?" So Jesus answered them, "My teaching is not mine, but his who sent me; if any man's will is to do his will, he shall know whether the teaching is from God or whether I am speaking on my own authority. He who speaks on his own authority seeks his own glory; but he who seeks the glory of him who sent him is true, and in him there is no falsehood."   John 7: 14-18

THE PRAYER FOR THE DAY

From being satisfied with myself, save me, good Lord. Burn into me the sight of the Cities of Dreadful Night and the City of Righteousness. Make me ever to hunger and thirst after righteousness. As I walk in mean streets, as I am importuned by beggars, as I walk with my friends, let impatience with the world make me patient to serve thee in any way, however lowly; let discontent with modern life make me content to bear some part of the sorrows of the world. O Christ our Savior, Man of Sorrows and King of Glory, ever leading us from darkness to light, from evil to goodness, ever calling us and recalling us from earth to heaven, let me count all things but loss that I may be found in thee, and be numbered among those who follow thee whithersoever thou goest. Amen.[9]

BISHOP KEN

A young lady in a youth camp made the not uncommon request, "Please help me understand this Bible verse. There is so much in the Bible I cannot understand." This queried observation is quite like that of Mark Twain, who struggled for a time with the mysteries of Scripture, but finally came clear and wrote, "It is not what I do not understand in the Bible that bothers me; it is what I do understand." God's Word teaches us that we learn to understand and to know his will by studying it in the Scriptures and by doing it in everyday living. There is a sense in which Christianity is a "do-it-yourself" growth in grace, for it invites us to learn the teachings of Jesus by practicing them daily.

The doctor or the minister learns the practice of his profession in internship and through his vocation. He may know his theories and lessons very well when he graduates from school, but he becomes a doctor or a pastor as he practices his profession in the service of people. A mechanical engineer becomes involved in long study, but he receives his engineering status as he utilizes his knowledge in planning and programming machines that can serve people. The same principle applies to Christian living. A Christian begins to do God's will as he has come to know it in the Bible, and in the daily practicing of his faith his knowledge of God becomes clearer and greater. Luther explains it in his *small catechism* in this way, "The good and gracious will of God is done indeed without our prayer; but we pray . . . that it may be done also among us."

THE LORD'S PRAYER

41

SECOND TUESDAY IN LENT

Learn not to be defeated by the immediate.

The Scripture

But a Pharisee in the council named Gamaliel, a teacher of the law, held in honor by all the people, stood up and ordered the men to be put outside for a while. And he said to them, "Men of Israel, take care what you do with these men. For before these days Theudas arose, giving himself out to be somebody, and a number of men, about four hundred joined him; but he was slain and all who followed him were dispersed and came to nothing. After him Judas the Galilean arose in the days of the census and drew away some of the people after him; he also perished, and all who followed him were scattered. So in the present case I tell you, keep away from these men and let them alone; for if this plan or this undertaking is of men, it will fail; but if it is of God, you will not be able to overthrow them. You might even be found opposing God!"

So they took his advice, and when they had called in the apostles, they beat them and charged them not to speak in the name of Jesus, and let them go. Then they left the presence of the council, rejoicing that they were counted worthy to suffer dishonor for the name. And every day in the temple and at home they did not cease teaching and preaching Jesus as the Christ.
Acts 5: 34-42

THE PRAYER FOR THE DAY

Lord, let me be ever courteous and easie to be entreated; never let me fall into a peevish or contentious spirit, but follow peace with all men, offering forgiveness, inviting them by courtesies, ready to confess my own errors, apt to make amends and desirous to be reconcil'd. Let no sickness or cross accident, no imployment or weariness make me angry or ungentle, and discontented or unthankful or uneasie. Give me the spirit of a Christian, charitable, humble, merciful, and meek, useful and liberal, complying with every chance, angry at nothing but my own sins, and grieving at the sins of others. That while my passion obeys my reason, and my reason is religious, and my religion is pure and undefiled, managed with humility, and adorn'd with charity, I may dwell in thy love, and be thy son and servant for ever, through Jesus Christ our Lord. Amen.

THOMAS Á KEMPIS

42

There are many men, whose names we know well, who are involved in the history of early Christianity. But one man seldom noted by name but widely acclaimed by precept is Gamaliel, the New Testament "doctor of law." Gamaliel is like an elder statesman, who repeatedly counseled with wise restraint. He brought to any setting a sense of balance, and asked that all sides of a situation be carefully reviewed before decision or action were taken. He had an inner serenity that contributed an outer poise.

How many times haste tries to force a solution to a problem or perplexity when the moderating influence of time would give the matter better perspective and greater simplicity. Wise counsel usually says, "Give time a chance. Wait and see what happens." Or as Gamaliel has put it, "If this plan or this undertaking is of men, it will fail; but if it is of God, you will not be abble to overthrow them."[a]

How will this consideration affect people? What are its implications for a period of time? Is there an eternal perspective to be remembered? These are Gamaliel-like questions that may be involved in decision making.

Life needs both Gamaliels and Peters; the Gamaliels will give life stability and steadiness, and the Peters will give life alertness to opportunity and leadership for action. Both temperaments are important to life and wise is the person who will practice the patience of Gamaliel.

THE LORD'S PRAYER

---

[a] Acts 5:38, 39

> *To write the biography of a Christian is like trying to record the history of a fragrance—the fragrance of the knowledge of Jesus.*

The Scripture

"What do you think? A man had two sons; and he went to the first and said, 'Son, go and work in the vineyard today.' And he answered, 'I will not;' but afterward he repented and went. And he went to the second and said the same; and he answered, 'I go, sir,' but did not go. Which of the two did the will of his father?" They said, "The first." Jesus said to them, "Truly, I say to you, the tax collectors and the harlots go into the kingdom of God before you. For John came to you in the way of righteousness, and you did not believe him, but the tax collectors and the harlots believed him; and even when you saw it, you did not afterward repent and believe him."

Matthew 21: 28-32

THE PRAYER FOR THE DAY

Accept the work of this day, O Lord, as we lay it at thy feet. Thou knowest its imperfections, and we know. Of the brave purposes of the morning only a few have found their fulfilment. We bless thee that thou art no hard taskmaster, watching grimly the stint of work we bring, but the Father and Teacher of men who rejoices with us as we learn to work. We have naught to boast before thee, but we do not fear thy face. Thou knowest all things and thou art love. Accept every right intention, however brokenly fulfilled, but grant that ere our life is done we may under thy tuition become true master workmen who know the art of a just and valiant life. Amen.[10]

WALTER RAUSCHENBUSCH

There are two kinds of hypocrisy. There are those who pretend to be better than they are, and there are those who are better than they pretend to be. The Scripture here illustrates this truth by the parable of two sons. Both sons were unsatisfactory people. One made an impressive profession but seemed to refute it by his personal performance. The other contributed a significant practice far exceeding his open profession.

Jesus once spoke sharply about the first classification when he said like this, "And in the hearing of all the people he said to his disciples, 'Beware of the scribes, who like to go about in long robes, and love salutations in the market places and the best seats in the synagogues and the places of honor at feasts, who devour widows' houses and for a pretense make long prayers. They will receive the greater condemnation.'"[a] He was severe with the pretenders, who wore masks of propriety, which covered their wayward actions. These people put on an external display of piety, to hide their inconsistent living.

Surprisingly enough there are others who practice Christianity in daily living beyond their public profession. Oftentimes these people appear to be hardheaded materialists, who somehow enjoy doing kind and generous things almost in secret as if they were ashamed of them. Often these people live more Christian lives than many professing Christians. Undoubtedly the second class of hypocrisy is much to be preferred to the former, for fine promises can never take the place of performance, nor can fine words ever become a substitute for fine deeds. The ideal Christian life seeks to have profession and practice match, for the mark of a Christian is in obedience, both in word and deed.

THE LORD'S PRAYER

---
[a] Luke 20:45-47

> *Not what happens to us matters most, but what happens in us.*

The Scripture

So, passing by Mysia, they went down to Troas. And a vision appeared to Paul in the night: a man of Macedonia was standing beseeching him and saying, "Come over to Macedonia and help us." And when he had seen the vision, immediately we sought to go on into Macedonia, concluding that God had called us to preach the gospel to them.

Setting sail therefore from Troas, we made a direct journey to Samothrace, and the following day to Neapolis, and from there to Philippi, which is the leading city of the district of Macedonia, and a Roman colony. We remained in this city some days; and on the sabbath day we went outside the gate to the riverside, where we supposed there was a place of prayer; and we sat down and spoke to the women who had come together. One who heard us was a woman named Lydia, from the City of Thyatira, a seller of purple goods, who was a worshipper of God. The Lord opened her heart to give heed to what was said by Paul. And when she was baptized, with her household, she besought us, saying, "If you have judged me to be faithful to the Lord, come to my house and stay." And she prevailed upon us.   **Acts 16: 8-15**

THE PRAYER FOR THE DAY

Lord, I know not what I ought to ask of thee; thou only knowest what I need; thou lovest me better than I know how to love myself. O Father! give to thy child that which he himself knows not how to ask. I dare not ask either for crosses or consolations: I simply present myself before thee, I open my heart to thee. Behold my needs which I know not myself; see and do according to thy tender mercy. Smite, or heal; depress me, or raise me up: I adore all thy purposes without knowing them; I am silent; I offer myself in sacrifice: I yield myself to thee; I would have no other desire than to accomplish thy will. Teach me to pray. Pray thyself in me. Amen.

FRANCOIS DE LA MOTHE FENELON

How clearly the will of God was revealed to Paul in the vision in the Macedonia cry, "Come over to Macedonia and help us."[a] It was comparatively simple to discern the purpose and the providence of divine leading in this request.

Most of the time the divine purpose is not so clearly stated. In fact, there is real temptation to look upon life as completely impartial and to believe that life treats all exactly the same, regardless of any faith in Providence. Like the cynic we are tempted to say, "All things come alike to all people." There is birth and death, joy and sorrow, tragedy and triumph. An earthquake takes its toll among all people without respect to personal faith. A plane crash obliterates the lives of all. Three crosses were on Calvary's hill. On two of the crosses were thieves; and on the central cross, Christ, but all three were crucified. The crucifixion on Good Friday must have seemed a most purposeless event in history.

But while all things may come alike to all people, all things do not come out alike. As time passes the divine plan and purpose take form. It is in retrospect that the purposes and patterns of God become plain. The Cross became God's way to accomplish his redemption for humankind. Christians cannot easily make the statement, "This is God's will for me," except as they seek to have a knowledge of his will in the revelation of himself in Jesus. An openness to God with an eager mind, purified by the discipline of prayer, expectantly alert to the promptings and call of his Holy Spirit, is the surest way to have a vision of his highest. "We know that in everything God works for good with those who love him."[b] and in that confident faith he makes visible to us his will in the common events of any day.

THE LORD'S PRAYER

---

[a] Acts 16:9
[b] Rom. 8:28

47

Fall to your knees! Humble yourself before God, for he hears before you call. He knows your loneliness, for he felt it on the cross, and he knows human need, for he bought it on Golgotha.

The Scripture

And one does not take the honor upon himself, but he is called by God, just as Aaron was.

So also Christ did not exalt himself to be made a high priest, but was appointed by him who said to him, "Thou art my Son, today I have begotten thee;" as he says also in another place, "Thou art a priest for ever, after the order of Melchizedek."

In the days of his flesh, Jesus offered up prayers and supplications, with loud cries and tears, to him who was able to save him from death, and he was heard for his godly fear. Although he was a Son, he learned obedience through what he suffered; and being made perfect he became the source of eternal salvation to all who obey him, being designated by God a high priest after the order of Melchizedek.   Hebrews 5: 4-10

THE PRAYER FOR THE DAY

Lord, I know not what is before me this day, but thou knowest. I desire to leave all in thy hands, and to place myself at thy disposal. Do for me as thou seest best. Prosper me in all I undertake. Give me good success if it be thy will. But, if thou seest that crosses and disappointments are better for me, give me grace to accept them as from thee. Enable me to bear them meekly and cheerfully, and to say, Father, not my will, but thine, be done. O my God, make me happy this day in thy service. Keep my conscience void of offense. Let me do nothing, say nothing, desire nothing, which is contrary to thy will. Give me a thankful spirit. O for a heart to praise thee for all that thou hast given me, and for all thou hast withheld from me. Amen.[11]

ASHTON OXENDEN

About the Lesson

Jesus' patience with difficult situations and with the necessity of suffering came from his absolute trust in the eternal purposes of God. His life task was to accomplish the will of God, who sent him, and to bring to completion his earthly mission of salvation. Therefore, Jesus suffered patiently, endured courageously and gave his life faithfully in acknowledgment of "not my will, but thine, be done."[a]

Three times we read that there were tears on the face of Jesus. He wept at the grave of Lazarus, tears of loving sympathy. He wept as he saw Jerusalem and the tribulations through which that city was to pass. He shed tears in the Garden of Gethsemane as his holy life quelled in the prospect of hanging upon the cross. Thus the eternal Son of God knew what subjection and surrender meant as he became a pilgrim upon the path of suffering and rejection.

Is it not true that sooner or later some form of trouble or trial comes to everyone and evokes one or two reactions? Either it embitters and hardens life, with the person resentful and cynical, or it enriches and ennobles life, making one gentle and more compassionate. The difference between the two is the trust in God on the inside of the person himself. "My ship is so little and the sea so big," but it can stand steady in a time of storm, if anchorage is faith in the Master.

The Lord's Prayer

---

[a] Luke 22:42

49

Augustine said, "Love God and do whatever you please," for if you love God you will not do anything to wound him.

The Scripture

"Hear another parable. There was a householder who planted a vineyard, and set a hedge around it, and dug a wine press in it, and built a tower, and let it out to tenants, and went into another country. When the season of fruit drew near, he sent his servants to the tenants, to get his fruit; and the tenants took his servants and beat one, killed another, and stoned another. Again he sent other servants, more than the first; and they did the same to them. Afterward he sent his son to them, saying, 'They will respect my son.' But when the tenants saw the son, they said to themselves, 'This is the heir; come, let us kill him and have his inheritance.' And they took him and cast him out of the vineyard, and killed him. When therefore the owner of the vineyard comes, what will he do to those tenants?" They said to him, "He will put those wretches to a miserable death, and let out the vineyard to other tenants who will give him the fruits in their seasons."

Jesus said to them, "Have you never read in the scriptures: 'The very stone which the builders rejected has become the head of the corner; this was the Lord's doing, and it is marvelous in our eyes?'"   Matthew 21:33-42

THE PRAYER FOR THE DAY

Almighty and most merciful Father, in whom we live and move and have our being, to whose tender compassion we owe our safety in days past, together with all the comforts of this present life, and the hopes of that which is to come; we praise thee, O God, our Creator; unto thee do we give thanks, O God, our exceeding joy, who daily pourest thy benefits upon us. Grant, we beseech thee, that Jesus our Lord, the hope of glory, may be formed in us, in all humility, meekness, patience, contentedness, and absolute surrender of our souls and bodies to thy holy will and pleasure. Leave us not, nor forsake us, O Father, but conduct us safe through all changes of our condition here, in an unchangeable love to thee, and in holy tranquillity of mind in thy love to us, till we come to dwell with thee, and rejoice in thee forever. Amen.[12]

SIMON PATRICK

This parable is so crystal clear that even the details in it have a meaning. It has three major thrusts. It speaks about the character of God. God trusts men to do his will just as the owner of the vineyard entrusted its care to the cultivators. God has infinite patience, like the master in the vineyard, who sent messenger after messenger with a final appeal by sending his own son. God is just! Even as the vineyard was ultimately taken away from the careless cultivators and given to others, so God may place our responsibilities in other hands if we fail him in doing them as we ought. When a man is useless to God he is at the lowest possible level.

This parable speaks about man. It emphasizes human privilege. God gives men not only tasks but the skills and ability to do them. Just as the master of the vineyard permitted the cultivators to do their tasks in their way, so God likewise allocates to each one his work for his day. The parable indicates the deliberateness of human sinfulness. The cultivators disobeyed the master, and sin is disobeying God's command. It is deliberately living life in our way rather than in His.

The parable also reveals Jesus. It shows quite clearly how the son came after a succession of messengers, who came as servants. Jesus came as a son. In the parable the hands of wicked men killed the son, just as men did the worst they could think to do to Jesus and hung him on a cross where he gave his life "a ransom for many."[a]

THE LORD'S PRAYER

---

[a] Mark 10:45b

Wide open are thy hands,
    Paying with more than gold
The aweful debt of guilty men,
    Forever and of old.
Ah, let me grasp those hands,
    That we may never part,
And let the power of their blood
    Sustain my fainting heart.

Wide open are thine arms,
    A fallen world to embrace;
To take to love and endless rest
    Our whole forsaken race.
Lord, I am sad and poor,
    But boundless is thy grace;
Give me the soul-transforming joy
    For which I seek thy face.

Draw all my mind and heart
    Up to thy throne on high,
And let thy sacred Cross exalt
    My spirit to the sky.
To these, thy mighty hands,
    My spirit I resign;
Living, I live alone to thee,
    Dying, alone am thine.

Ascribed to St. Bernard of Clairvaux, 1091-1153
Tr. Charles Porterfield Krauth, 1823-83

ACCEPT THE HELP OF HIS HANDS

The Scripture

> Then he said to Thomas, "Put your finger here, and see my
> hands; and put out your hand, and place it in my side; do not
> be faithless, but believing."   John 20:27

Hands are a fascinating study. It has been said that if the
faces in da Vinci's painting of the Last Supper were covered,
the characters could be identified by the hands. The psalmist
has written, "I hold my life in my hand." Hands do tell a tale.

Even handshaking can be a revealing experience. Here is a
hand that is stiff and straight; it communicates very little in
the way of friendship or cordiality. It is like greeting a piece
of cardboard. Or here is another hand that is like clasping a
wet dish cloth. This hand is soft and belongs to someone who
works indoors; while here is another hand that is firm and
strong and must belong to someone who does manual work
with tools. Hands have their own language. They can be folded
in prayer or closed hard into a fist by resentment, rebellion,
or pain. See hands and you see something of the person himself.

A famous sculptress, has said, "Whether your hands are
beautiful does not depend on tapering fingers or smooth skin.
It depends on what is in your heart, and what your soul and
mind make your hands do." Anyone can make of his hands
the hands of guilt or the hands of goodness. Jesus said of
Judas, "The hand of him who betrays me is with me on the
table."[a] What you do with your hands indicates something
of the quality of your soul.

The hands of Jesus must likewise be a revelation. They
were the hands of a laborer and a craftsman; they busied themselves during boyhood days in a carpenter's shop. They were

---

[a] Luke 22:21

hands that grew strong and sturdy fashioning furniture for the homes of his time and making the yoke for oxen of the fields. Perhaps saddles were constructed for camels. Jesus' hands had to be steady and sure.

The hands of Christ served people. It was his hands that lifted little children to the attention of mankind. The blessing of his hands multiplied the food to feed the multitude. His hands were stretched forth to heal the one suffering from leprosy, as well as to give sight to blind Bartimaeus. Simon Peter gladly grasped those hands the night he walked on the waters and was rescued by them from the devouring deep.

Through the centuries Christ has been the great healer for humanity. His touch has still its ancient power, for the imperfect and unclean in any life can be made pure. Life's heavy burden can be wonderfully lightened, and the night of fear can be done away by the touch of his hand. He remains the great physician for body, mind and spirit.

By his hands, Christ hung on the cross. The hands of Christ are different from our hands! He bears in them the print of nails. Those hands ever remind us that he gave his life on Calvary's cross, that forgiveness and healing might come to this world. Hubert Simpson has told of a little girl, who, returning from school one day, caused concern in her home, telling that she had been punished by her teacher for the first time in her life. Pressed to give the reason for her punishment, she confessed to a particularly grave fault. "But you never did a thing like that!" her mother queried. "No, of course, I didn't," the girl replied, "but no one would own up to it and someone had to, and so I held up my hand."[13] That is what happened on Calvary. Something had to be done about human sin and sinfulness, and the Lord held up his hands for our sake. No one ought misunderstand the pierced hands of love!

The saving hands of Jesus tell us eloquently in the words of the Apostle Paul, "Do you now know that your body is a temple of the Holy Spirit within you, which you have from

God? You are not your own; you were bought with a price. So glorify God in your body."[b] The price of the purchase was the suffering, crucifixion, and death on the cross. The bleeding hands of Christ are there to invite us to let them weave the patterns of our lives.

No person belongs to himself, for everyone belongs to someone or something. It is the height of stupidity to pretend that you are your own. A good father may say that he belongs to his family; a dedicated teacher will say that she belongs to her pupils, and an artist will acknowledge that he is owned by his art. Everyone has some kind of commitment.

How tragic to be wrongly possessed! When life's purpose is not worthy of your ultimate concern, when it causes fragmentation instead of cohesiveness, or invites to evil instead of to good, the basic dedication is wrong. More important than what belongs to a person is what the person belongs to. Not what he controls but what controls him, not what he masters but what masters him, not what he owns but what owns him is ultimately the essence of any life.

The real commitment of life cannot be concealed, for its marks are upon a person by what he thinks, says, and does. "You can tell a person by the company he keeps," is another way of saying that our associations, investments of time, and real loyalties identify us. The kind of soil through which a river flows stains the water and for hundreds of miles downstream announces the fact to everyone. A painter wears on his overalls splashes of the color he has been using during the past days. Even so, our lives are living epistles read by others of companionships enjoyed and of real commitments made. Paul could exclaim that a Christian person need not shout what he is from the housetops; it can be seen by men, for "I bear in my body the marks of Jesus."[c]

A little girl, accompanied by her father, was busy picking

---
[b] 1 Cor. 6:19-20
[c] Gal. 6:17

multi-colored flowers in a field. Suddenly she hurried over toward a number of particularly beautiful blossoms growing right on a river's bank. Her father quickly cautioned her about reaching for those flowers, explaining to her that at that particular place, the river, in making a turn, had undercut the bank and what looked like solid ground was really a cleft of earth overhanging the water. Said the father, "If you pick those flowers, you will make the bank and the flowers fall into the swirling stream and perhaps fall into the river yourself." How often are not many seemingly attractive associations as superficial and lacking in real worth as this undercut bank of the river. After this explanation the little lady turned to her father and asked, "What flowers may I pick?" To which the father replied, "You may pick as many flowers as you can reach without letting go of my hand." As many associations may be kept, as many investments of life made, and as many loyalties cherished, as may be had not letting go of the Master's hand.

A central appeal of Jesus Christ is his pierced hands. They are eloquent invitation. You belong to the Master! You have been bought with a price. You belong to One able to gather life together and to make it whole, worthy enough to make life meaningful with truth, beauty, peace, purpose, and love, and durable enough to hold it steady and strong amidst the turbulence and tempest of a storm-tossed existence!

The hands of Christ are sovereign hands. The hands that were held up by the cross are now lifted up in power, for the authority of those hands can be discerned in history and in human lives. Those hands used the Greek world with its common language and intellectual curiosity for proclaiming the gospel; they used the Roman world with its sense of empire for communicating the gospel into outlying areas; and they used the Hebrew world as creator of the setting which would give the gospel universal expectancy.

See those sovereign hands preparing a little lad in the city of Tarsus with fine schooling and careful academic training, so that later when Saul became Paul, he could blaze a trail of Christian truth across the Roman Empire. Those hands raised up a Luther, a Wesley, a Zwingli, so that an old world held hard under the heavy hand of ecclesiastical oppression might be made strangely free. Note those hands helping Albert Schweitzer off his organ bench and away from European acclamation to go to awakening Africa, where multi millions awaited the proclamation of the gospel and the planting of the church.

Much more difficult it is to discern his mighty hands in our time. Perhaps they are leading all peoples into a deeper yearning for peace and better race relations. Perhaps they are drawing the Christian denominations together so that the good news may be proclaimed with greater unity and coherence. Perhaps they are urging ecumenical conversations, so that the Christian message may come with greater force and fortune while open doors of opportunity prevail. Perhaps the deep need of humankind for physical relief is yet another way in which those mighty hands will use human hands and generous hearts to do his will in this day.

Auguste Rodin has sculptured a huge hand out of a block of marble, and in the hollow of that hand he has placed little forms that appear to be emerging from the stone. These little forms, representing human life, seem so secure and safe when held in that great strong huge hand. The sculpture seems to say in stone what God has said in his Word, "See my hands."[d]

When an old guide in the Alps saw a man trembling on the edge of a great crevice, he reached down a strong reassuring hand. "Here," he said, "take this hand. It has never yet lost a man." To the person of faith, battling amidst fearful days, God reaches down his hand and says, "Behold, I have graven

---

[d] John 20:27

you on the palms of my hands."[e] M. Louise Haskins has put the same thought this way, "Go out into the darkness and put your hand into the hand of God. That shall be to you better than light and safer than a known way."

> "The hands of Christ
>   Seem very frail
> For they were broken
>   By a nail.
>
> "But only they
>   Reach heaven at last
> Whom these frail, broken
>   Hands hold fast."

Jesus said, "See my hands," and seeing them, Thomas exclaimed, "My Lord and my God!"[f]

[e] Isaiah 49:16
[f] John 20:28

> *God walks into your soul with silent step. He comes to you in the sacraments and in his Word so undramatically with gentle yet persistent grace.*

The Scripture

Therefore gird up your minds, be sober, set your hope fully upon the grace that is coming to you at the revelation of Jesus Christ. As obedient children, do not be conformed to the passions of your former ignorance, but as he who called you is holy, be holy yourselves in all your conduct; since it is written, "You shall be holy, for I am holy." And if you invoke as Father him who judges each one impartially according to his deeds, conduct yourselves with fear throughout the time of your exile. You know that you were ransomed from the futile ways inherited from your fathers, not with perishable things such as silver or gold, but with the precious blood of Christ, like that of a lamb without blemish or spot. He was destined before the foundation of the world but was made manifest at the end of the times for your sake. Through him you have confidence in God, who raised him from the dead and gave him glory, so that your faith and hope are in God.   Peter 1: 13-21

THE PRAYER FOR THE DAY

Eternal God, we bow before thee in praise and adoration. For all thy goodness and mercy we thank thee, but above all for him, whom thou hast given to us, who sharing our nature humbled himself to share our own.

May we see him human as we are, knowing from within our temptations and struggles, sharing our manhood, wearing our flesh, living in our circumstances, crowning human life forever with his glory. May we know him also, the Son of God, revealing thy nature, bearing our sins, carrying our cross, making intercession for us, the Savior of our lives.

Made proud that he would suffer, too, like us, may we be made humbled, so that we may live like him. Amen.[15]

LESLIE WEATHERHEAD

This passage of Scripture mentions several characteristics of the Christless life and three characteristics of a Christ-filled life. The pagan life may be identified by ignorance, sensuality, and frustration, while the Christ-filled life bears the marks of obedience, reverence, and love.

Anyone unrelated to Jesus Christ must constantly guess and grope after the unknown God. "It is hard," said Plato, "to investigate and to find the framer and the father of the universe." Without Christ, God is ever a mystery. Christ came into a world that was characterized as a sensuous civilization, with life becoming a futile affair, spent like a shadow.

But for one to whom Christ has come, life is like the freshness of the morning and the dawning of a new day, full and enriched in many ways. It is characterized by wholesomeness, which is another word for "holiness," which is God's gift. With something of the purity of God in his life, a Christian is filled with wonder as he lives with a sense of the presence of God. He knows that he is a traveler on a way that has an eternal destiny, and that his life is infinitely precious because it has been redeemed by Jesus Christ. It must not be squandered. This Christ-filled life spills itself out in amity, good will, and loving regard. God is love, and the Christian life reflects, projects, and communicates this love everywhere.

THE LORD'S PRAYER

Life becomes insipid when it has no great love and is infested with passivity. God is a consuming fire, and we are puny embers.

The Scripture

And he called to him the twelve, and began to send them out two by two, and gave them authority over the unclean spirits. He charged them to take nothing for their journey except a staff; no bread, no bag, no money in their belts; but to wear sandals and not put on two tunics. And he said to them, "Where you enter a house, stay there until you leave the place. And if any place will not receive you and they refuse to hear you, when you leave, shake off the dust that is on your feet for a testimony against them." So they went out and preached that men should repent. And they cast out many demons, and anointed with oil many that were sick and healed them.

Mark 6: 7-13

THE PRAYER FOR THE DAY

Almighty God, I praise thee that I have wakened to the light of another earthly day; and now let me think of what a day should be. My days are thine, let them be spent for thee. My days are few, let them be spent with care. There are dark days behind me, forgive their sinfulness; there may be dark days before me, strengthen me for their trials. I pray thee to shine on this day, the day which I may call my own. Lord, as I go to my daily work, help me to take pleasure therein. Show me clearly what my duty is, help me to be faithful in doing it. Let all I do be well done, fit for thine eye to see. Give me strength to do, patience to bear, let my courage never fail. When I cannot love my work, let me think of it as thy task, and by my true love to thee make unlovely things shine in the light of thy great love; through the Lord Jesus Christ. Amen.

In this generation when we are "dress conscious" and often enjoy listing the ten best-dressed men or women, and most of us delight in our well-filled wardrobe and spend considerable time worrying about whether our attire is high fashion and "chic," the orders of Jesus, given his disciples when he sent them out as his ambassadors, seem strange and disturbing.

How simple were their needs. The person living in Palestine at the time of Jesus dressed with utter simplicity, wearing a tunic, which was little more than a cassock made out of sackcloth, an outer garment, called a "himation," which served as a cloak by day and a covering by night. A girdle or belt was worn to hold the tunic and cloak together, and was also a money belt. The headdress was a piece of cloth about a yard square and placed around the head to protect the eyes and neck from the glare of the sun. Sandals were on the feet, and a staff was held in the hand. Thus the first representatives of the gospel went forth in simplicity, in complete trust, and in a spirit of generosity.

This picture of the first ambassadors of Christ becomes bothersome amidst the affluence, luxury, and super abundance of America. Almost too painful are the words of Jesus, "If any man would come after me, let him deny himself, take up his cross daily and follow me."[a] The words "deny" may sometimes be translated "delete" or "forget." Is our Christian stewardship a matter of convenient giving, or does it involve some of the elements of sacrifice by which discipleship, the real stuff of Christianity, has lived? There were no cushions on the cross!

THE LORD'S PRAYER

(a) Luke 9:23

What we keep for ourselves is ultimately lost. What is lost for the sake of Christ, we may keep eternally.

The Scripture

A dispute also arose among them, which of them was to be regarded as the greatest. And he said to them, "The kings of the Gentiles exercise lordship over them; and those in authority over them are called benefactors. But not so with you; rather let the greatest among you become as the youngest, and the leader as one who serves. For which is the greater, one who sits at table, or one who serves? Is it not the one who sits at table? But I am among you as one who serves.

"You are those who have continued with me in my trials; as my Father appointed a kingdom for me, so do I appoint for you that you may eat and drink at my table in my kingdom, and sit on thrones judging the twelve tribes of Israel."

Luke 22: 24-30

THE PRAYER FOR THE DAY

O God, we praise thee for friends, that thou hast set us in families and in nations. We bless thee for all the power friendship has to gladden the heart and strengthen life, and the opportunities it offers to minister to others, even as others have ministered to us. May we praise thee with a kindly heart toward all races and conditions of men, an earnest desire to help in their advancement, and a refusal to take advantage of their necessities. May brotherhood sing thy praise by making war as abhorrent to us as it is to thee. Hasten the day, we pray thee, when mankind shall be one great family, worshiping the Father of us all and devoted to the common good; and to thy name shall be the glory and dominion now and forevermore. Amen.[16]

CHARLES WOLCOTT MERRIAM

Greatness among men is like a human pyramid. If more people must serve us than we must serve, we are counted to be important and socially significant. If someone should attain a position at the top of this pyramid, where everyone must serve and acclaim him, and, in turn, he needs acknowledge no one, this person is given the title, "greatest in the life of the world."

Greatness in the sight of God is like an inverted pyramid. If a person can serve more people with his life than in turn serve him, he is achieving some of the fulfillment in life about which Jesus spoke. If he can move down very close to the apex of the inverted pyramid, where Christ is, who upholds all of mankind, then he has achieved greatness in the sight of the Eternal. Greatness in God's eyes wears the guise of a servant.

Christian life is founded on the philosophy of giving. We give because Christ first gave himself. His love constrains us. Whittier talks about "the dear delight of doing good," and Abraham once said that he would be a blessing. It is God's Law of life that service leads to greatness. The higher a man really rises before others, the greater servant he must be. If we share in bearing the burdens of humanity by having a redemptive mission in life, there will follow satisfaction to ourselves, sunshine on the pathways of others, and a smile on the face of God.

THE LORD'S PRAYER

> *People who pray are the light bearers in any land. Add yourself to this bright company.*

The Scripture

And he arose and left the synagogue, and entered Simon's house. Now Simon's mother-in-law was ill with a high fever, and they besought him for her. And he stood over her and rebuked the fever, and it left her; and immediately she rose and served them.

Now when the sun was setting, all those who had any that were sick with various diseases brought them to him; and he laid his hands on every one of them and healed them. And demons also came out of many, crying, "You are the Son of God!" But he rebuked them, and would not allow them to speak, because they knew he was the Christ.

And when it was day he departed and went into a lonely place. And the people sought him and came to him, and would have kept him from leaving them; but he said to them, "I must preach the good news of the kingdom of God to the other cities also; for I was sent for this purpose." And he was preaching in the synagogues of Judea.   Luke 4: 38-44

THE PRAYER FOR THE DAY

Come, O Lord, in much mercy down into my soul, and take possession and dwell there. A homely mansion, I confess, for so glorious a Majesty, but such as thou art fitting up for the reception of thee, by holy and fervent desires of thine own inspiring. Enter then, and adorn, and make it such as thou canst inhabit, since it is the work of thy hands. Give me thine own self, without which, though thou shouldst give me all that ever thou hast made, yet could not my desires be satisfied. Let my soul ever seek thee, and let me persist in seeking, till I have found, and am in full possession of thee. Amen.

ST. AUGUSTINE

Christian life needs the renewing miracle of moments of solitude. Often the Master rose early in the morning so that he could be alone. It is written of him, "And after he had dismissed the crowds, he went up into the hills by himself to pray."[a] The most memorable such occasion is the Garden of Gethsemane experience, when he prayed to know and to accept the Father's will.

Every life needs to know the ministry of the strength in which our lives are held. "Be still, and know that I am God,"[b] is a prayer that lets life see a lighted candle and a high altar with a cross on it. Before a person meets others, he had best first meet God in prayer.

But Christian living involves more than prayer. It also involves service. Florence Alshorn, a great teacher, once directed a training school for fulltime Christian workers. She soon learned to know well human nature, and she had little time for students who suddenly discovered that their quiet hour for prayer always came at the time when dishes were to be washed. Pray we must, but prayer must never be an escape from the demands of reality. A Christian is a permeator of society and an answer to human need, rather than a separator from it.

Prayer can prepare us to rise from our knees to become "the good news" to others. If we have been the recipients of health and strength, of gifts and skills, they have been given us for use in service to others. Each of us can be the answer to the prayer, "Thy will be done, on earth as it is in heaven."[c]

THE LORD'S PRAYER

---

[a] Matt. 14:23
[b] Psalm 46:10
[c] Matt. 6:10

> *Let the unwearied and tender love of Christ to me make*
> *my love unwearied and tender to others.*

The Scripture

> For I think that God has exhibited us apostles as last of all,
> like men sentenced to death; because we have become a spec-
> tacle to the world, to angels and to men. We are fools for
> Christ's sake, but you are wise in Christ. We are weak, but
> you are strong. You are held in honor, but we in disrepute.
> To the present hour we hunger and thirst, we are ill-clad and
> buffeted and homeless, and we labor, working with our own
> hands. When reviled, we bless; when persecuted, we endure;
> when slandered, we try to conciliate; we have become, and are
> now, as the refuse of the world, the offscouring of all things.
> I do not write this to make you ashamed, but to admonish
> you as my beloved children. For though you have countless
> guides in Christ, you do not have many fathers. For I became
> your father in Christ Jesus through the gospel. I urge you,
> then be imitators of me.   Corinthians 4:9-16

THE PRAYER FOR THE DAY

Lord of love, we look to thee in humble prayer.

Thou who didst perfect on the cross a redemptive work for
all, grant that our lives may be redemptive. Teach us, O Lord,
the deeper meaning of sacrifice, so that our living will lead
not to exhaustion but to renewal of spirit.

May the hungry be fed, the sick healed, the aged sustained;
may little children grow up in safety and happiness, and youth
follow after bright visions of a fuller life.

Crown thy mercies in us with the gift of greater wisdom,
wider sympathies and more faithful following of thy com-
mands. Touch our spirits with thine, and direct us into paths
of right and peace. Thy kingdom come, O Lord, in the com-
monplaces of our lives. In markets and factories, legislative
halls, churches, schools and homes, may thy will be done, to
the well-being of all men and to the glory of thy name.
Through Jesus Christ our Lord. Amen.

In the Sunday worship of many parishes the congregation sings,

> "We give thee but thine own,
> Whate'er the gift may be;
> All that we have is thine alone,
> A trust, O Lord, from thee."

It is the same language the Apostle Paul uses when he says, "What have you that you did not receive?"[a] In this simple question there is a glimpse of the shining beauty of God's grace.

All that we have and are and hope to be are God's bequests. When we remember all that God has done for us, our pride falls and humble gratitude rises. It is easy to forget that we are debtors and that God is the most lavish and generous giver of all, even to offering his Son on the cross.

Paul uses a whiplash of words to deflate our pride, our smugness, our sense of superiority in this luxury-satiated existence in America. With scathing irony Paul reminds all Christians that the Christlike life involves humble service, a willingness to carry the cross, and if need be, death for Christ's sake. He uses the imagery of a slave beaten and of life insulted, as being fit demeanor for the Christian. This conduct, so uninviting from the standpoint of the world, can be used as a part of the infinite wisdom of God.

The signs of great sacrifice can be seen on most everything we have, if we look closely. Life's supreme achievements usually have marks of martyrdom on them. They come to us out of someone's tribulation. Everyday convenience, a good heritage and Christian privilege cannot be taken for granted. They have been bought with other blood than ours. What do we have, that we did not receive at cost to someone else?

THE LORD'S PRAYER

---

[a] 1 Cor. 4:7

"Praise ye and bless the Lord, and give thanks unto him, and serve him with great humility."

The Scripture

Then I looked, and I heard around the throne and the living creatures and the elders the voice of many angels, numbering myriads of myriads and thousands and thousands, saying with a loud voice, "Worthy is the Lamb who was slain, to receive power and wealth and wisdom and might and honor and glory and blessing!" And I heard every creature in heaven and on earth and under the earth and in the sea, and all therein, saying, "To him who sits upon the throne and to the Lamb be blessing and honor and glory and might for ever and ever!" And the four living creatures said, "Amen!" and the elders fell down and worshiped.   **Revelation 5: 11-14**

THE PRAYER FOR THE DAY

We praise Thee, O God, we acknowledge thee to be the Lord.
All the earth doth worship thee, the Father everlasting.
To thee all Angels cry aloud; the Heavens, and all the
  Powers therein;
To thee Cherubim and Seraphim continually do cry,
Holy, Holy, Holy, Lord God of Sabaoth;
Heaven and earth are full of the Majesty of thy glory.
The glorious company of the Apostles praise thee.
The goodly fellowship of the Prophets praise thee.
The noble army of martyrs praise thee.
The holy church throughout the world doth acknowledge
  thee;
The Father, of an infinite majesty;
Thine adorable, true, and only Son;
Also the Holy Ghost, the Comforter.
Thou art the King of Glory, O Christ,
Thou art the everlasting Son of the Father.
O Lord, save thy people, and bless thine heritage.
Govern them, and lift them up for ever.
O Lord, let thy mercy be upon us, as our trust is in thee.
O Lord, in thee have I trusted; let me never be confounded.
                              From the Te Deum Laudamus

70

Have you ever watched the director of a symphony orchestra as he leads his musicians in the playing of mighty music? From one chord to another and from one musical phrase to others, he leads his musicians in unfolding majestic melody. Often the music moves ever higher, until finally it reaches a triumphant and unforgettable conclusion.

So with our Christian religion. It has great music in it, which moves from experience to experience, through smiles and tears, to make its final harmony of praise. The psalmist writes in the One Hundred Forty-sixth Psalm, "I will praise the Lord as long as I live; I will sing praises to my God while I have being."[a]

Praise is a part of any Christian's total life. It helps us live in the summertime of faith and invites us to remember, more than the clouds, the blue skies of life. It fixes our attention not on the sad, sorry schemes of living, but on the goodness and greatness of God.

Praise is appropriate for the difficult times in life, too. In your trials and tribulations, "Praise ye the Lord!" In your illnesses and defeats, "Praise ye the Lord!" In your darkness and bereavements, "Praise ye the Lord!" This is faith's victory.

Praise and adoration and worship are great helpers and healers. When life is too much with us and we feel wounded in spirit, depressed and dull in disposition, and cynical and bitter in our attitudes, praise comes along to start a song in our hearts and to sustain a Christian mood of joy. Like great music that mounts ever higher, so let praise carry us ever closer to him, who is entitled to blessing and honor and glory and might forever and ever!

THE LORD'S PRAYER

---

[a] Psalm 146:2

Thousand times by me be greeted,
  Jesus, who hast loved me,
And thyself to death submitted
  From my treason against thee:
Ah, how happy do I feel,
When 'fore thee I humbly kneel,
See thee on the cross expiring,
And true life for me acquiring.

Jesus, thee I view in spirit,
  Covered o'er with blood and wounds:
Now salvation through thy merit
  For my sin-sick soul abounds:
O who can, thou Prince of Peace,
Who didst thirst for our release,
Fully fathom all that's treasured
In thy love's design unmeasured?

Heal me, O my soul's Physician,
  Whersoe'er I'm sick or sad;
All the woes of my condition
  By thy balm be now allayed:
Heal the hurts which Adam wrought,
Or which on myself I've brought;
If thy blood me only cover,
My distress will soon be over.

With the deepest adoration
  Humbly at thy feet I lie,
And with fervent supplication
  Unto thee for succour cry:
My petition kindly hear;
Say in answer to my prayer,
"I will change thy grief and sadness
Into comfort, joy, and gladness."

12th Cent. St. Bernard of Clairvaux
1653 P. Gerhardt
1754 J. Gambold, a.
From the Moravian Hymn Book

FOLLOW THE WAY OF HIS FEET

The Scripture

> "See my hands and my feet, that it is I myself; handle me, and see; for a spirit has not flesh and bones as you see that I have."   **Luke 24:39**

In this age of travel, including the extraordinary and astounding feats of outer space travel, it can still be safely said that the feet of Jesus have traveled more miles than those of any person. At first, the feet of Jesus were like those of anyone else, baby feet, then the feet of a child walking and climbing the rugged and rough terrain of Palestine. They became the feet of a young man who visited home, synagogue, and workshop. They were the feet of the Master in his public ministry, walking many roads, like the rock-studded way from Jerusalem to Bethlehem, or the winding trail past the home of Mary and Martha to Jericho, or the wider, easier road to Emmaus. The feet of Jesus were pinioned with nails to the cross, so that his feet, like his hands, bear the marks of crucifixion. They have traveled a greater distance than those of any other because they have continued even today to cross the frontiers of human life and to influence and to transform civilization and culture, some place in every country in the world except two, Afghanistan and Tibet.

In Isaiah's prophetic recitation about the Suffering Servant, those blessed feet of the Savior are called "beautiful." "How beautiful upon the mountains are the feet of him who brings good tidings, who publishes peace, who brings good tidings of good, who publishes salvation, who says to Zion, 'Your God reigns.' "[a]

No one can really escape those feet, no matter how hard he tries, for they are persistent and patient feet, constantly seeking to make known the Redeemer. Just as God walked in

---

[a] Isaiah 52:7

73

the cool of the day in the Garden of Eden and called, "Where are you?"[b] so the relentless feet of Christ keep after us, wanting us, seeking us for himself. Those inescapable feet will find us, hunt us down, and bring us captive into the fellowship of the Christian family, if we but let them.

Unhappy, rebellious Francis Thompson has called Christ "The Hound of Heaven," and has written about him in these words:

> I fled him down the nights and down the days;
> I fled him down the arches of the years;
> I fled him down the Labyrinthine ways
> Of my own mind; and in the midst of tears
> I hid from him, and under running laughter,
>   Up vistaed hopes I sped;
>   And shot, precipitated,
> Adown titanic glooms of chasméd fears,
> From those strong feet that followed, followed after.
>
> But with unhurrying chase
> And unperturbéd pace,
> Deliberate speed, majestic instancy,
> They beat — and a Voice beat
> More instant than the feet —
> "All things betray thee who betrayest Me."
>
> Ah fondest, blindest, weakest
> I am he whom thou seekest!
> Thou drivest Love from thee who drivest Me![17]

We might as well try to escape the air we breathe or the ground on which we walk as to try to escape the love of God abroad in the universe, becoming his thought in our hearts, his image in our minds, or his voice in our souls.

His invitation is to follow in the way of his feet, and to participate in his footprints, which blaze trails as life's great pioneer. He has built roads with his life down which we are invited to walk.

Often I love to seek out a little byway, far away from the

---

[b] Gen. 3:9

speeding traffic and the noise and whirl of wheels on our great super highways. These little trails, many times just tracks, bring you easily and quickly into the woods for communion with the quiet of nature and the peace of the countryside. How restful is the experience of wending a quiet way! Here nature can be orderly and lovely, and its special converse appreciated and understood. Oftentimes these seldom-traveled paths wind their way past fast-running streams and placid lakes to the home of some seasoned old seer. Roads are significant because of where they lead. Robert Frost, our renowned poet, has written this very well in these words,

> I shall be telling this with a sigh
> Somewhere ages and ages hence.
> Two roads traveled in a wood, and I,
> I took the one less traveled by
> And that made all the difference.[18]

Follow the way of his feet to Bethlehem. This is the way of beginning and awakening. It speaks the language of wonder, awe, and reverence. In Bethlehem the Almighty God becomes incarnate in Jesus Christ, and we are ushered into his presence. Self moves out of the scene, and Jesus Christ becomes the source and center of all achievement and the goal of all desire. To know his nature, to receive his life, and to live by his mercy become our obsession and gladness.

Most of the time in this present nuclear and satellite age man's achievement is emphasized and glory is given to men. At times there is temptation to paraphrase the Twenty-third Psalm, "Science is my shepherd. I shall not want." Often our living becomes egocentric to the full, so that the writer to the Hebrews accurately pictures man's modern plight, when he says, ". . . Now in putting everything in subjection to man, he left nothing outside his control. As it is, we do not yet see everything in subjection to him. But we see Jesus . . ."[c]

---

[c] Heb. 2:8

Can it be determined that life today needs a direction beyond what man himself can provide? Is not the refrain, "glory to man," altogether superficial and inadequate?

Every age has its own problems, its own burdens and complexities. Charles Malik, the distinguished statesman-professor, who has served as a foreign ambassador to Washington and a representative of Lebanon to the United Nations, has catalogued our present-day deterioration like this, "Nervousness, fear, cowardice, rebelliousness, absence of peace, flattening of thought and feeling, absence of the dimension of depth, disintegration of community, massive irrationality, weakening of the sense of personal responsibility, denial of the invisible and spiritual, the proud self-sufficiency of man."[19] Amidst this modern welter of sin, Bethlehem comes with its invitation for man with all his bruises to trust himself to the mercy of God. Jesus is a Savior from this kind of sin.

Beyond the sins of society, each man has his own soul to worry about. Is he master of himself? Is he at peace with himself? Is he true to himself? Is he true to Christ? How deeply does he know the power of the living God in his own life? Has he forgiven his brother — really forgiven him? Are all rancor and resentment in his daily living washed away?

Follow the way of his feet to Jericho. This is the way of service, for it was on this much-traveled road that the good Samaritan became Scripture's lesson to all of us. On this road the Christian learns by doing. Jesus said, "He that doeth my will shall know," and in that promise he requests us to let our professions coincide with our practices. Here the highest self is selfless and Christ becomes vital and alive, as a person becomes helpful to the need of someone else.

Men have always asked the question, "What shall I do with my life?" and many are the answers that have been given in reply. But suppose human answers be pushed aside and we turn to him who lived life completely and beautifully and harmoniously. Suppose we turn to him who was the master of life and ask him, "What shall I do with my life? What is the secret to the mystery of living? What is the key I can use to unlock the entanglements of my existence?" Listen! That Master turns to us and says, "He who is greatest among you shall be your servant."[d]

This answer squares with truth, no matter where we turn. Go into the world of nature, seek out a grainfield and find the blade of wheat that has the finest grain in it. An inexperienced person may pick out a stalk of grain that stands straight and strong and tall and say, "That must be wheat that counts." But a wizened old farmer, going over to a stalk of grain that is bending so low that it almost touches the ground, will say to us, "There you will have kernels of wheat that are valuable." And so with human life. Not a life lifted high in pride, but a life that is bent low in humility and service counts.

Take a sunbeam, and send it through a spectroscope. See the colors of the rainbow: red, orange, yellow, green, blue, indigo, and violet. That sunbeam falls on a blade of grass and the grass says, "I'll take green and give it back to people. The other six colors disappear, and the grass can keep green because it promises to give it away. The sunbeam falls on a rose, and the rose says, "I'll take red and reflect that, so when people see me, they will see the crimson of beautiful scarlet. The other six colors disappear, and the rose can keep red because it promises to give it away. The sunbeam falls on a white flower, and this flower says, "I'll take all seven colors and give them back to life," and it can keep all seven, because it promises to give them away. What we are willing to share of what we are and of what we have, in a spirit of selfless service, that we can keep, but that which we seek to keep for ourselves we lose. Our Master once said, "He who finds his life will lose it, and he who loses his life for my sake will find

---

[d] Matt. 23:11

it."[e] Other familiar words have it like this, "For every one who exalts himself will be humbled, and he who humbles himself will be exalted."[f] [20]

Follow the way of his feet to Emmaus. How dejected Cleopas and another disciple were as they walked this way after the crucifixion and the burial at the borrowed tomb. All they had to remember was a futile hope, an old wound, and a dream grown dim. Then they heard the footsteps of Jesus as he walked with them on the way and knew that he was alive again. The joy of it was beyond hoping. Everything became alive again. Jesus lives, and dreams become real! Jesus lives, and life has a glow again! Jesus lives, and others must know! Gladly they had fellowship with each other because of him and hurried to tell the other disciples, only to discover that he was also there, and that all of them were now members of a redemptive fellowship because of Christ.

Follow the way of his feet, which the whole Christian family on earth travels, for it goes on and on fulfilling Christ's redemptive purposes among men, bearing all races and all nations, including Christians in Asia, Africa, Europe, and the Americas, toward the eternal city. It is this redemptive fellowship that has the task of communicating Christianity to the world, and this challenge is increasingly an unfinished assignment, since the birth rate in the world is faster than the rebirth rate into the Christian family. God forbid that this redemptive fellowship ever become an introverted experience, occupied with maintaining its own existence rather than with giving its life away, like the Master did, to fulfill its mission and eternal destiny.

On the Emmaus Road each person gains a sense of divine vocation. The witness of any Christian in the place where he lives and works is an unprecedented opportunity. This witness may take many forms: integrity in business, a forgiv-

---
[e] Matt. 10:39
[f] Luke 14:11

78

ing spirit, a social conscience, a good word spoken for his church, simple kindliness, naming the name of Jesus. This is primarily a service of being rather than of doing. It is a ministry of reconciliation. Jesus said, "You are the salt of the earth."[g] — salt, not of the church, but of the earth. Salt fulfills its function only as it is first gathered and cleansed, and then scattered to season and serve. Here is a parable of the Emmaus Road experience. In the presence of Jesus, listening to his word, receiving the sacraments, a Christian is cleansed and empowered and then scattered into the secular world to become salt and light to other people. Any Christian is a witness by how he prays and what he says, by how he gives and lives, and by what he is!

Follow the way of his feet to Calvary. It is difficult to explain the full meaning of following the way to the Cross. Human words lag and drag and break down in trying to express the inexpressible, for it is unthinkable that the pure, holy, loving Son of God should give his life on a tree. The finest of Christian scholarship, all of Christian experience and the best of Christian insight for centuries past have not been able fully to fathom the depth of the meaning of the Cross.

Sometimes the Cross is explained as representing a ransom. Jesus gave his life "as a ransom for many."[h] Just as one prisoner was sometimes exchanged for another and occasionally a captain was exchanged for a number of prisoners, so this King of kings gave his life in ransom for all humankind.

Some have explained the Cross on the basis of government. Nothing interferes with life so much as the presence of evil in human relationships, and no one has handled this power of evil as has Jesus. His cross destroys, through love, the power of Satan. Christ rules the world from the wood.

Who can estimate the amount of dedicated living that the way of the cross has inspired? Look what love has done on

---

[g] Matt. 5:13
[h] Mark 10:45

the Cross and see the compulsion of that divine compassion expressing itself in persons. Without Calvary there would have been no Carey or Livingstone or Schweitzer. From the Cross comes power to live dedicated lives.

Still others have followed his feet to Golgotha and have called the Cross, "Life's greatest substitution." Barrabas and every man can say, "His feet walked instead of mine. He took my place. He died for me." Christ put on our sandals to set us free from our sins.

Certainly the Cross stands for reconciliation. When our wayward feet wander into the far country, away from the Father's heart and purpose, the Cross like a magnet attracts them back to his fellowship and to him. Men are prodigals until the Cross reconciles them to God.

Follow the way of his feet to know something of the length and the breadth and the height and the depth of God's eternal love in Christ Jesus.

With faith in God what ought to be done, can be done.

The Scripture

On the next day the people who remained on the other side of the sea saw that there had been only one boat there, and that Jesus had not entered the boat with his disciples, but that his disciples had gone away alone. However, boats from Tiberias came near the place where they ate the bread after the Lord had given thanks. So when the people saw that Jesus was not there, nor his disciples, they themselves got into the boats and went to Capernaum, seeking Jesus.

When they found him on the other side of the sea, they said to him, "Rabbi, when did you come here?" Jesus answered them, "Truly, truly, I say to you, you seek me, not because you saw signs, but because you ate your fill of the loaves. Do not labor for the food which perishes, but for the food which endures to eternal life, which the Son of man will give to you; for on him has God the Father set his seal." Then they said to him, "What must we do, to be doing the work of God?" Jesus answered them, "This is the work of God, that you believe in him whom he has sent." John 6: 22-29

THE PRAYER FOR THE DAY

O Lord, in these difficult times, when there is a seeming opposition of knowledge and faith, and an accumulation of facts beyond the power of the human mind to conceive; and good men of all religions, more and more, meet in thee; and the strife between classes in society, and between good and evil in our own souls, is not less than of old; and the love of pleasure and the desires of the flesh are always coming in between us and thee; and we cannot rise above these things to see the light of heaven, but are tossed upon a sea of troubles — we pray thee be our guide and strength and light, that, looking up to thee always, we may behold the rock on which we stand, and be confident in the word which thou hast spoken. Amen.

BENJAMIN JOWETT

About the Lesson

On another occasion Jesus stated today's lesson in these words, "Do not lay up for yourselves treasures on earth, where moth and rust consume and where thieves break in and steal, but lay up for yourselves treasures in heaven, where neither moth nor rust consumes and where thieves do not break in and steal. For where your treasure is, there will your heart be also."[a]

Here Jesus pleads for a proper sense of values. "Work for the food which lasts, and which gives eternal life," is his insistent plea. Keep your earth-bound point of view in its proper place; a man may be the richest person on earth, as far as things are concerned, and yet have a haunting dissatisfaction and an unrequited longing within his heart.

Jesus, as the bread of life, satisfies our hunger for truth, for he himself is truth. He satisfies our longing for love, for he himself is love. We search for life, and he has come to give it more abundantly, for he is much stronger than sin or death. These are the real heart-hungers of the human soul, and Christ Jesus alone can satisfy the need.

Feed your mind with the truth of God, purge the imagination with his beauty, open the heart to his love, devote the will to his purposes, and life will become refreshed, fed, and satisfied by the food which the Son of Man alone is. Life eternal is to know him!

The Lord's Prayer

---

[a] Matt. 6:19-21

83

FOURTH TUESDAY IN LENT

Jesus Christ fills the hungry with good things.

The Scripture

So they said to him, "Then what sign do you do, that we may see, and believe you? What work do you perform? Our fathers ate the manna in the wilderness; as it is written, 'He gave them bread from heaven to eat'." Jesus then said to them "Truly, truly, I say to you, it was not Moses who gave you the bread from heaven; my Father gives you the true bread from heaven. For the bread of God is that which comes down from heaven, and gives life to the world." They said to him, "Lord, give us this bread always."

Jesus said to them, "I am the bread of life; he who comes to me shall not hunger, and he who believes in me shall never thirst." John 6: 30-35

THE PRAYER FOR THE DAY

Once more a new day lies before us, our Father. As we go out among men to do our work, touching the hands and lives of our fellows, make us, we pray thee, friends of all the world. Save us from blighting the fresh flower of any heart by the flare of sudden anger or secret hate. May we not bruise the rightful self-respect of any by contempt or malice. Help us to cheer the suffering by our sympathy, to freshen the drooping by our hopefulness, and to strengthen in all the wholesome sense of worth and the joy of life. Save us from the deadly poison of class-pride. Grant that we may look all men in the face with the eyes of a brother. If any one needs us, make us ready to yield our help ungrudgingly, unless higher duties claim us, and may we rejoice that we have it in us to be helpful to our fellow men. Amen.

WALTER RAUSCHENBUSCH

This is one of the notable passages in the Gospel of John, for it is more than simply a lovely statement. It holds within it the deeper meaning of God's message to us. In a profound sense Jesus is the bread of life in that he sustains living which is more than mere physical existence. Real living is relationship with God, and this life of obedience and love is induced, nourished, and sustained by Jesus Christ. Jesus becomes the essential in giving to any and to all real life, full, free, and founded in God.

Jesus comes as the "bread of life" in his Word and in the sacraments. These are the priceless treasures of the church. His coming to us establishes a new relationship with God, so that we are one with him. In him we live and move and have our being. His invitation is extended without any reservations to all who are willing to receive it. God loves us to himself in His Son, Jesus Christ.

Today there are thousands upon thousands of people in the world seeking for bread to sustain physical life, but more important, seeking for bread that feeds the whole life of man. When Jesus ascended to heaven, he gave his disciples the command to tell others about the "bread of life." These disciples did tell others, who in turn became ambassadors, and thus the cycle was repeated again and again, until we are the torchbearers of faith to people in our community, nation and world.

Any offering in the church is an opportunity to bring the "bread of life" to people in today's world. Any offering plate in a Christian church is really a flying saucer encompassing the globe, bringing its cargo of "good news" wherever it can and to whom it may.

THE LORD'S PRAYER

FIFTH WEDNESDAY IN LENT

The greatest gift is not silver or gold but the gift of oneself.

The Scripture

And he sat down opposite the treasury, and watched the multitude putting money into the treasury. Many rich people put in large sums. And a poor widow came, and put in two copper coins, which make a penny. And he called his disciples to him, and said to them, "Truly, I say to you, this poor widow has put in more than all those who are contributing to the treasury. For they all contributed out of their abundance; but she out of her poverty has put in everything she had, her whole living."

Mark 12: 41-44

THE PRAYER FOR THE DAY

Almighty God, our heavenly Father, from whom cometh every good and perfect gift, we call to remembrance thy loving kindness and thy tender mercies which have been ever of old, and with grateful hearts we lift up to thee the voice of our thanksgiving. Stir up, we beseech thee, O Lord, the wills of thy faithful people, that we who have freely received of thy bounty may of thy bounty freely give; through Jesus Christ, our Lord. Amen.[21]

86

When the offering plate was being passed, Jesus watched the contributions that were placed on it. There is something about our giving which identifies us. You can learn about a person, if you can see how he invests his money. The old quotation may be paraphrased this way, "Where your money goes, there your heart is."

As the offering plate was watched, contributions in varying amounts were placed in it, and the discerning eyes of the Master detected that some of the smaller contributions in amount were really large, while other gifts were given only out of superabundance. The might of the mite by the poor widow speaks very eloquently about stewardship.

Real giving must have something of sacrifice about it. The amount of the gift does not matter nearly so much as the cost of the contribution to the giver. Again, real giving has something of the recklessness of faith in it. When contributions are the result of giving only that which is reasonable and proper and when there is nothing of faith in the willingness of God to supply the larder, stewardship has lost some of its luster.

The veteran colored parson used to say, "The more I keep giving, the more the Lord keeps giving to me." What we give is only that which we have first received; the Lord has promised, "Give, and it will be given to you; good measure, pressed down, shaken together, running over, will be put into your lap."[a] Cold and calculated contributions so often reveal a miscalculating Christian.

Real giving can begin only when first of all we have given ourselves to Jesus Christ and have put all that we have and are at his disposal. What he can do with us when he is in complete control is beyond our imagination.

THE LORD'S PRAYER

---

[a] Luke 6:38

87

I bind unto myself today the strong name of the Trinity, Father, Son and Holy Ghost.

The Scripture

Many of his disciples ,when they heard it, said, "This is a hard saying; who can listen to it?" But Jesus, knowing in himself that his disciples murmured at it, said to them, "Do you take offense at this?" Then what if you were to see the Son of man ascending where he was before? It is the spirit that gives life, the flesh is of no avail; the words that I have spoken to you are spirit and life. But there are some of you that do not believe." For Jesus knew from the first who those were that did not believe, and who it was that should betray him. And he said, "This is why I told you that no one can come to me unless it is granted him by the Father."

John 6: 60-65

THE PRAYER FOR THE DAY

Here are our lives, O thou great Creator God, who hast made the universe and stationed the stars in their courses. Thy handiwork is seen when thou madest man and didst breathe into him the very essence of thine own life.

Here are our lives, O Lord, frail, incomplete, often fearful, but our lives nonetheless. Teach us that they are so precious to thee that thou didst redeem them on the cross in the person of thy Son, Jesus Christ.

Here are our lives, Father, purchased with a great price and a love past finding out. May we both dedicate and use them to thy glory in the simple things of everyday existence like working and playing, learning and teaching, laughing and loving, that all may be to thy glory.

Grant that these days may strengthen our lives for thy great name's sake. Amen.

The disciples did not have difficulty in understanding what Jesus was saying to them. The trouble was in their willingness to accept his high and holy demands. Our Christianity becomes exceedingly difficult when we are to live it in daily life, for its ethical and moral demands are tremendous. Many a man has turned sadly away from the call of Christ in his life because the challenges and the disciplines have been too hard. He has not been willing to pay the price of practicing his confession.

The Christian life, like a river, appears small at its source and even uninviting, but as it is pursued, it becomes wider and deeper and more satisfying, finally to flow into the fullness of the beauty of God's eternity. The non-Christian life is just the opposite. It begins ostensibly and with great promise, but the farther that it is followed, the less satisfying it becomes, until finally it concludes itself in futility.

It is Christ who fills life full. Jesus, known and loved, brings a new spell over life, so that evil begins to droop and the best bursts into bloom. Christ restores broken relationships, so that what once seemed hopelessly broken and damaged is now completely healed. Christ lights up all of life with courage, serenity, and peace. He gives to anyone the limitless splendor of a divinely owned and ordered life.

THE LORD'S PRAYER

The Christian has confidence that God is with him amid the storms and stress of life.

The Scripture

But we have this treasure in earthen vessels, to show that the transcendent power belongs to God and not to us. We are afflicted in every way, but not crushed; perplexed, but not driven to despair; persecuted, but not forsaken, struck down, but not destroyed; always carrying in the body the death of Jesus, so that the life of Jesus may also be manifested in our bodies. For while we live we are always being given up to death for Jesus' sake, so that the life of Jesus may be manifested in our mortal flesh. So death is at work in us, but life in you.

Since we have the same spirit of faith as he had who wrote, "I believed, and so I spoke," we too believe, and so we speak, knowing that he who raised the Lord Jesus will raise us also with Jesus and bring us with you into his presence.

2 Corinthians 4: 7-14

THE PRAYER FOR THE DAY

O God of Grace, who hast called us to thine eternal glory in Christ our Lord; we praise and bless thy glorious name.
To see thee is to find meaning in life.
To obtain thy forgiveness is healing and peace.
To be thy servant is perfect freedom.
To meditate upon thy purpose and power is enduring hope.
To love and trust thee is to face life and death unafraid.
O heavenly Father, whom to know is life eternal; in thy great mercy open our eyes to thy glory and incline our hearts to do thy will; through Jesus Christ our Lord. Amen.[22]

ERNEST FREMONT TITTLE

How different people can be! For some people life seems dull and uninviting, and they become cynical and caustic. Listen to one of them, who writes like this, "I am up against a blank wall. Evenings are impossible. Most talk is banality. Life doesn't seem to have any purpose or meaning. Any mention of morality seems a strange kind of cantation."

Contrast this statement with the Apostle in the letter to the Ephesians: "Now to him who by the power at work within us is able to do far more abundantly than all that we ask or think, to him be glory in the church and in Christ Jesus to all generations, for ever and ever."[a]

What a difference in the perspective of these two persons! The aged Apostle, with every reason to be disgruntled and discouraged, is radiant, and the young man, with every reason to be content, is bitter. And the contrast between the two can be explained by the absence of genuine Christian faith in the life of the youth.

Christian life is not drab nor is it an escape from life or in any sense a liability. It is partnership with God, facing with him whatever life brings. It helps us by the mercy of God to shape our lives as a potter shapes a vase, and to face life unafraid and with our hearts uplifted. It gives wings to life, so that there is no yielding to fear, no enslavement by sin, and no destruction by despair. It is clear eyes ahead, a clean heart within, and a note of hope for the future.

THE LORD'S PRAYER

---

[a] Eph. 3:20-21

The Cross is life's most magnificent obsession.

The Scripture

And again he said to them, "I go away, and you will seek me and die in your sin; where I am going, you cannot come." Then said the Jews, "Will he kill himself, since he says, 'Where I am going, you cannot come'?" He said to them, "You are from below, I am from above; you are of this world, I am not of this world. I told you that you would die in your sins, for you will die in your sins unless you believe that I am he." They said to him, "Who are you?" Jesus said to them, "Even what I have told you from the beginning. I have much to say about you and much to judge; but he who sent me is true, and I declare to the world what I have heard from him." They did not understand that he spoke to them of the Father. So Jesus said, "When you have lifted up the Son of man, then you will know that I am he, and that I do nothing on my own authority but speak thus as the Father taught me. And he who sent me is with me; he has not left me alone, for I always do what is pleasing to him." As he spoke thus, many believed in him.

John 8: 21-30

THE PRAYER FOR THE DAY

Thou knowest, O heavenly Father, the duties that lie before me this day, the dangers that may confront me, the sins that most beset me. Guide me, strengthen me, protect me.

Give me thy life in such abundance that I may this day hold my soul in thy pure light. Give me thy power, that I may become a power for righteousness among my fellows. Give me thy love, that all lesser things may have no attraction for me; that selfishness, impurity, and falseness may drop away as dead desires, holding no meaning for me. Let me find thy power, thy love, thy life, in all mankind, and in the secret places of my own soul. Amen.

A BOOK OF PRAYERS FOR STUDENTS

Educationists sometimes tell us that a learning experience requires repetition of information at least three times. What infinite patience the Master had with men as he stated and re-stated his great insights and simple truths. Uncomplainingly he kept his pace slow and careful, so that inexperienced disciples might follow him, and yet when his teaching is done, his crucifixion becomes more effective and potent in announcing his suffering mission to men than all his prior telling of it. This statement is almost startling, "When you have lifted up the Son of man, then you will know that I am he, and that I do nothing on my own authority but speak thus as the Father taught me."[a]

Is it not amazing that a cross on a hill has proved the most central and unforgettable thing in history, and that this sign of death and failure has come unloosed as an irresistible power in all of life? Here is something more than man. This is God's grace, going the full length of complete love to redeem men from what they are. In the death of Christ on the cross is revealed how God thinks and speaks and acts toward sinful men. The Cross is there to help us live by faith in him who died on it.

THE LORD'S PRAYER

---

[a] John 8: 28

O sacred Head, now wounded,
  With grief and shame weighed down,
Now scornfully surrounded,
  With thorns, thine only crown;
O sacred Head, what glory,
  What bliss till now was thine!
Yet, though despised and gory,
  I joy to call thee mine.

How art thou pale with anguish,
  With sore abuse and scorn;
How does that visage languish,
  Which once was bright as morn!
Thy grief and bitter passion
  Were all for sinner's gain;
Mine, mine was the transgression,
  But thine the deadly pain.

What language shall I borrow
  To thank thee, dearest friend,
For this thy dying sorrow,
  Thy pity without end?
O make me thine for ever,
  And should I fainting be,
Lord, let me never, never
  Outlive my love to thee.

Be near when I am dying,
  O show thy Cross to me!
And, for my succor flying,
  Come, Lord, to set me free.
These eyes, new faith receiving,
  From thee shall never move;
For he who dies believing
  Dies safely in thy love. Amen.

Ascribed to St. Bernard of Clairvaux, 1091-1153
Paul Gerhardt, 1607-76
Tr. James Waddell Alexander, 1804-59 a.

SEE THE LOOK OF HIS FACE

The Scripture

> For it is the God who said, "Let light shine out of darkness,"
> who has shone in our hearts to give the light of the knowledge
> of the glory of God in the face of Christ.   2 Corinthians 4:6

In this age of scientific miracles we can see by television the faces of people who are many miles from us. Would it not be interesting to see the faces of people who lived centuries before us? Were that possible, surely one face, above all others, which we would want to see, would be the face of Christ. We do have his Words to hear, but what would it mean to look on his countenance? A deep human longing is to see "the kind look" of the Master. Each time the words of the benediction are said, "The Lord make his face shine upon thee," we are made conscious of the image of his face.

Why is it that we have portraits by artists of some of the contemporaries of Jesus but none of the Master himself? Perhaps the Jewish abhorrence for personal portraits has contributed to a lack of any authentic picture of Jesus. The oldest known reproduction of the figure of Christ, with five disciples about him, is on the chalice from Antioch, but that this craftsmanship dates back to the actual time of Christ is speculative. Others have suggested that St. Veronica's veil is real and is purported to have the face of Christ on it, since the time it was used to wipe his face while he carried the cross. But this appears to be only legendary. Our most publicized reports of paintings of the Master lack authenticity.

Perhaps the fact that there is no authentic likeness of the Son of God is a divine order of things, for we are invited to walk by faith and not by sight. Any portrayal of the Master would fall short of making him the Master of all men. On the cover of this book is Salvador Dali's "Christ of St. John of the Cross," which is an artist's conception of the Crucifixion, effective and yet inaccurate. In our home is Hoffman's "Christ at the Age of Twelve," before which picture an African youth paused and asked, "Who is this?" To him Christ wore a black face! Pictures of the Master painted in Kowloon, New Territories, Hong Kong, give him an Oriental face. Most of the famous portraits of the Master make him a Caucasian. Many have seen replicas of Thorwaldson's sculptured masterpiece, "Come unto me," which to be seen as it stands in the chancel of the cathedral in Copenhagen, Denmark, requires the observer to get on his knees, because the head is tilted and the face looks downward. Perhaps this is the posture from which we can begin to see the image of his face, which is veiled behind the curtain of twenty centuries, and which requires us to behold it by faith.

Strange, then, that the face of Jesus should be mentioned so often in Scripture. It must have been a face unlike any other, for St. John writes in the Book of Revelation that the reward for living a consecrated life will be the privilege "to see his face."[a] Perhaps few words in the Old Testament and the New are mentioned as often as the word "face." Often in the Bible the word "face" has a wider interpretation, meaning "presence."

To gaze upon the face of the Master, which is the gaze of faith, can become a transforming experience changing us in his presence, so that we may become like him. How long is it since your life came under the spell of deep and commanding inspiration? When last were you taken out of this world on the wings of unforgettable music, overaweing scenery, or an inspiring address? How long is it since the "Spirit himself (bore) witness with our spirit that we are children of God?"[b] Was it quiet reflection on God's Word or the harmony of a choir anthem, the resurgence of the resistless tide of spring, or the sounds of a great symphony, the moving

[a] Rev. 22:4
[b] Rom. 8:16

experience of marriage, or the outcry of the first little bundle of life that helped make all things new and sent life-like laughter looking for the Lord of all? Let us look then to the face of the Master to see there, "the light of the knowledge of the glory of God."

Notice some of the characteristics of that face as Scripture has given them to us. An old youth camp song phrases the invitation this way,

> Turn your eyes upon Jesus,
>   Look full in His wonderful face;
> And the things of earth will grow strangely dim
>   In the light of His glory and grace.[23]

First of all, his face was etched with the lines of struggle, "because his face was set toward Jerusalem."[c] Another version has it, in the New English Bible, "He set his face resolutely towards Jerusalem." Instead he might have journeyed to beautiful Galilee, where his home was and his friends, to the prospect for long years of subtle teaching and then to peaceful death at last. But instead he turned his face toward Jerusalem where death awaited him — awful death — when it became midnight at noonday, and human hatred for him was rampant and human hands were raised in malediction and even God seemed to flee. Yet, he set his face toward Jerusalem, to go to the cross. His face wore the marks of struggle. He was tempted in the wilderness, and all through his pilgrimage "like as we are;" his struggle can best be seen in the Gethsemane prayer, "If it be possible, let this cup pass."[d] The terrible tugs of temptation were real to him, for he lived a human life to the full, and anything less than this would be to turn his human existence into meaninglessness and his death on a cross into a sham. Jesus knew the struggles of our

---
[c] Luke 9:53
[d] Matt. 26:39

97

lives, for as he went to Jerusalem, his face "was like flint," his hands were clenched with the knuckles showing white, and the fingers clenched hard into the hand. Here was the struggle of the heart of the Son of Man laid bare. Even the disciples became afraid, because they loved him, and because they were fearful of what might happen to them.

How well Jesus knows our frame and our frailty, for he was one with us. He knows the heights and the depths, the sunshine and the shadows, the tragedies and triumphs that characterize human lives. He knows our struggles too, for he pioneered and blazed the trail of trial and tribulation. When passengers express concern about air travel, it becomes comfort for them to know that whatever comes, the pilot is in it with them, and that his life as well as the lives of the passengers is involved in anything that occurs. Of Jesus it can also be said, "He is in it with us," in all things knowing the full fury of life's demands.

Again, the Master had a radiant face. When he came down from the Mount of Transfiguration, Matthew reports, "His face shone like the sun."[e] Mark complements this luminous quality by stating, "His garment became glistening, exceeding white," and Luke adds, "His raiment became white and dazzling." While Gethsemane and Golgotha drew upon his countenance the deep claims of struggle, Hermon and Olivet revealed on that face a light not of this earth. Upon that face was reflected a spirit of perfect goodness. From within came the radiance of the divine. Here was no ordinary countenance, for though it knew struggle and temptation in all things like us, yet it had about it the sinlessness of the Savior. While it could have withering anger and scorn, it also had the tenderness that attracted little children and the peace of perfect faith. This countenance has been described as belonging to the Crystal Christ, in whom there was no shadow nor iniquity.

---

[e] Matt. 17:2

Jesus was the human face of God. Just as some persons become the very human incarnation of all that is evil with appearances that are ugly, with eyes that are sinister and features that are uninviting, so a complete contrast is the face of Jesus, so assured and compassionate, that John the Baptist says, "Behold, the Lamb of God, who takes away the sin of the world!"[f] The radiance of that face can melt us to penitence, comfort us in sorrow, stay us in temptation, encourage our faith in times of fear, eliminate pride and anger, vanish loneliness, and lead us onward in life's adventure, because it is radiant with a reflection of the divine.

The face of Jesus can be identified by the mark of sacrifice. In setting his face to go to Jerusalem, Jesus was traveling on the way to the cross. Even in the description of the crucifixion itself, as given us by Matthew, we are reminded that his face became involved in that awful ordeal. For Scripture reports, "Then they spat in his face, and struck him; and some slapped him, saying, 'Prophesy to us, you Christ! Who is it that struck you?'"[g] There is hardly another word except "grace" that describes love's sacrifice on Calvary's cross.

A common phrase is the one which states that self-preservation is the law of life; but it is true in a much more profound way than is ordinarily acknowledged. In every life there are many selves — the poorer self, the better self, the egocentric self, and the selfless self. Which self we determine to preserve indicates the kind of person we are. Dr. George A. Buttrick tells of two men who were walking down the stairs of a dry-cleaning shop, when one of the men accidentally dropped a lighted match into a pail of cleaning fluid. There was an instantaneous explosion of flame. One of the men hurried out the nearest exit to save himself, and the other ran quickly to warn the workers on the other floors of what had happened. Each was determined to preserve his real self. Yes, self-

---

[f] John 1:29
[g] Matt. 26:68

preservation is a law of life, but which self do we intend to preserve?[24]

In the world in which we live any real progress or advancement involves sacrifice. Good students give themselves to their studies by relentless discipline; real teachers shed the blood of mental struggle; mothers pour out a faithful vigil in love; any person giving himself completely for a great goal does not talk about sacrifice but is gladly involved in a deep dedication. The measure of the commitment determines the amount of the sacrifice. Love is given in response to a full obedience. On this deep stratum, suppose the question is raised: If someone were totally committed to sacrifice, even to the point of crucifixion on a cross, would this not be redemption complete and full? Is this not the character of the face that hangs in crucifixion on the cross? To see this face is more than to look. It is to become involved and to hear again the words, "If any man would come after me, let him deny himself and take up his cross and follow me."[h] While we can never fully achieve this kind of obedience, we can grow toward it. A Christian life serves as it moves from opportunity to opportunity, not in triumph but in love.

The face of Christ shines with the glory of an eternal quality, for on it was the glory of God. It is in his countenance that we find peace and in the light of his life that rest is given. We find we "are being changed into his likeness from one degree of glory to another."[i] St. John announces the same conviction when he says, "It does not yet appear what we shall be, but we know that when he appears we shall be like him, for we shall see him as he is."[j]

A modern poet has penned into words the experience of one who was dying. Family and friends were gathered about to

---

(h) Mark 8:34
(i) 2 Cor. 3:18
(j) 1 John 3:2

console and to await the angel of death. The dying person spoke like this,

> "Shapeless and grim,
> A Shadow dim
> O'erhung my ways,
> And darkened all my days.
> And all who saw,
> With bated breath,
> Said, 'It is Death!'

> "And I, in weakness,
> Slipping towards the Night,
> In sore affright
> Looked up. And lo! —
> No Spectre grim,
> But just a dim
> Sweet face,
> A sweet high mother-face,
> A face like Christ's own Mother's face,
> Alight with tenderness
> And grace.

> " 'Thou art not Death,' I cried —
> For Life's supremest fantasy
> Had never thus envisaged Death to me;—
> 'Thou art not Death, the End!'

> "In accents winning,
> Came the answer — 'Friend,
> There is no Death!
> I am the Beginning,
> — Not the End.' "[25]

"For now we see in a mirror dimly, but then face to face. Now I know in part; then I shall understand fully, even as I have been fully understood."[k] When the Lord lifts his countenance upon us, he gives us peace everlasting.

See the look of his face!

(k) 1 Cor. 13:12

Divine love in action is accomplished in Christ and finished by his cross, but is a constantly continuing action through his life-giving spirit.

The Scripture

Now the point in what we are saying is this: we have such a high priest, one who is seated at the right hand of the throne of the Majesty in heaven, a minister in the sanctuary and the true tent which is set up not by man but by the Lord. For every high priest is appointed to offer gifts and sacrifices; hence it is necessary for this priest also to have something to offer. Now if he were on earth, he would not be a priest at all, since there are priests who offer gifts according to the law.

Hebrews 8: 1-4

THE PRAYER FOR THE DAY

O Lord our God, we worship thee, and give thanks to thee for the precious gift of life thou hast given us. We thank thee that thou hast opened our eyes to the revelation of thyself in thy word, and hast called us into the fellowship of Christ.

We confess that we have followed the selfish devices of our own hearts, have listened to the voice of the world, and have marred thy image in us by purposes and plans thou couldst not own. Have mercy upon us, O Lord, and of thy goodness forgive us.

Attend us, O Lord, in all our doings: in the work and leisure of the common day. Fix in our hearts thy eternal purposes, that we may not waste our efforts in vain striving, but may know now thy peace which passeth all understanding.

We commend to thy loving care all those who are dear to us either in family or friendship. Grant thy mighty protection to those in any kind of danger; deliver us all from fear through knowledge of thy perfect love which casteth out fear. We pray too, for our enemies. Teach us the mind of Christ in dealing with them.

Guide our country; further the quest for peace among the nations. Purify and enliven thy church throughout the world that she may faithfully and powerfully declare the good news of salvation, through Jesus Christ our Lord. Amen.

Doors are an interesting study and indicate something about the dwelling to which they invite admission. A dilapidated, ill-fitting door usually means a poor dwelling, while a beautifully-designed, well-painted door usually indicates an attractive house or building. Doors are even more significant, however, because they provide access to something. Jesus once said, "I am the door."[a] What a beautiful door he is! But even more wonderful: he provides entrance and access to God himself.

One of the great affirmations of the Christian faith is that God is directly approachable through Jesus Christ. In Christ we have free access to divine love. No additional mediator or intercessor is necessary, for Christ has become the perfect priest, once and for all becoming the bridge between God and man. The Cross of Calvary is the perfect sacrifice, which has linked the depth of human need with the height of divine love.

The Old Testament stressed man's achievement, while the New Testament announces Christ's atonement. The sacrifice of Christ at Golgotha is the surety or guarantee of this open and free availability of grace for all. Furthermore, the Old Testament priesthood had nothing of permanency about it, for it involved human death and was constantly resupplied, while the priesthood of Jesus Christ is eternal and never passes away. In this sense Jesus becomes indispensable for every man, for "no one comes to the Father, but by him."[b] He is ever at the service of men and thus becomes a complete Savior for all. He opens the door to the fellowship and friendship of God for every man.

THE LORD'S PRAYER

---

[a] John 19:9
[b] John 14:6

God is almost shy for he calls us in humility and with patience.

The Scripture

After this Jesus went about in Galilee; he would not go about in Judea, because the Jews sought to kill him. Now the Jews' feast of Tabernacles was at hand. So his brothers said to him, "Leave here and go to Judea, that your disciples may see the works you are doing. For no man works in secret if he seeks to be known openly. If you do these things, show yourself to the world." For even his brothers did not believe in him. Jesus said to them, "My time has not yet come, but your time is always here. The world cannot hate you, but it hates me because I testify of it that its works are evil. Go to the feast yourselves; I am not going up to the feast, for my time has not yet fully come." So saying, he remained in Galilee.

John 7: 1-9

The Prayer for the Day

O God, give us strength to live another day. Let us not turn coward before its difficulties or prove disobedient to its duties. Let us not lose faith in our fellow men. Keep us sweet and sound of heart, in spite of ingratitude, treachery, or meanness. Preserve us from minding little stings, or giving them. Help us to keep our hearts clean, and to live so honestly and fearlessly that no outward failure can dishearten us or take away the joy of conscious integrity. Open wide the eyes of our souls that we may see good in all things. Grant us this day some new vision of thy truth, inspire us with the spirit of joy and gladness, and make us cups of strength to suffering souls; in the name of the strong Deliverer, our only Lord and Savior, Jesus Christ. Amen.

Time is one of life's greatest values. Each of us has been given sixty diamond seconds in every golden hour of the fleeting day. How we invest the time given us determines in a measure who and what we are. Daily schedules indicate the priorities in our lives for which we are willing to spend time.

Jesus teaches in the lesson for this day not only the importance of utilizing the time alloted to us, but also the great significance of timing. There is a best time, a most suitable opportunity, a most appropriate circumstance, for the accomplishment of God's purposes. Jesus teaches us that he accomplishes his will not in man's time but in God's time. Often our impatience must learn to await God's wisdom. His acts are done according to his timetable. In the fullness of time down the corridor of the years comes the voice of a Savior in the cry of a Baby, in sermons from a boat, and in a prayer from a Cross, "Father, forgive them." Will we hear him now?

When we are bitter and biting; when evil seems to have the stronger hand and pride possesses too much power; when faith is failing and love is trodden in the dust; when we serve our own interests and plan only for ourselves — then may the Son of God, the Savior of Men, and the Sovereign of all speak to us so clearly and tenderly that we will hear his voice and permit him to have his way and will in our lives!

THE LORD'S PRAYER

All I could never be, all men ignored in me, this I was worth to God.

The Scripture

When he had gone out, Jesus said, "Now is the Son of man glorified, and in him God is glorified; if God is glorified in him, God will also glorify him in himself, and glorify him at once. Little children, yet a little while I am with you. You will seek me; and as I said to the Jews so now I say to you, 'Where I am going you cannot come.' A new commandment I give to you, that you love one another; even as I have loved you, that you also love one another. By this all men will know that you are my disciples, if you have love for one another."

John 13: 31-35

THE PRAYER FOR THE DAY

Thou God of Love and Mercy, we pray before thee in the tender mercies of Calvary. Forgive us for taking thy mercy lightly, glancing at the Cross for a brief time, only to pass on and be as we were. May we have more love for thee, thou Savior of men, as we reach through time and distance to ponder Golgotha's deepest shadows.

O Lord, give us forgiving and forgiven hearts. Help us with faces turned toward the Cross to witness thy saving love to people with new power. Comfort those in need of thy solace. Give renewed health to all who are ill in body, mind, or soul. Give peace to troubled lives. Forgive us our sins, and let righteousness and mercy shine through us to thy glory. Grant this in the name of Jesus. Amen.

An old catechism asks the question, "What is the chief end of man?" and makes this answer, "The chief end of man is to glorify God and to enjoy him for ever."

Jesus had a threefold glory. His first glory was in the Cross, for by it was revealed the supremacy of divine sacrifice. Life quickly forgets the successful person, but it remembers the sacrificial soul. The greater the sacrifice, the greater the remembrance and the glory.

Jesus gave God glory. The perfect way for anyone to indicate trust and love is by obedience. A national leader is honored when his people follow his direction; a parent is complimented through obedient children, and Jesus glorified God by becoming obedient to his will, even through death on a cross.

By the Cross Jesus was glorified. After the Crucifixion came the Resurrection, the Ascension, and ultimately his complete triumph. The exaltation of Christ follows his humiliation; his coronation in glory follows his crucifixion. The Cross becomes an eternal crown.

In his valedictory Christ gave his farewell command, in which he announced his love for his disciples and indicated that this was the final test of discipleship: that they love one another even as he had loved them. In his farewell address Jesus asked his followers to demonstrate forgiveness and compassion to all men and thereby give glory to God.

THE LORD'S PRAYER

Life's greatest resource is a victorious spirit sustained by a faith in Christ which never grows dim.

The Scripture

If the worshipers had once been cleansed, they would no longer have any consciousness of sin. But in these sacrifices there is a reminder of sin year after year. For it is impossible that the blood of bulls and goats should take away sins.

Consequently, when Christ came into the world, he said, "Sacrifices and offerings thou hast not desired, but a body hast thou prepared for me; in burnt offerings and sin offerings thou hast taken no pleasure. Then I said, 'Lo, I have come to do thy will, O God,' as it is written of me in the roll of the book." When he said above, "Thou hast neither desired nor taken pleasure in sacrifices and offerings and burnt offerings and sin offerings" (these are offered according to the law), then he added, "Lo, I have come to do thy will." He abolishes the first in order to establish the second. And by that will we have been sanctified through the offering of the body of Jesus Christ once for all. **Hebrews 10: 2-10**

The Prayer for the Day

O God, whose blessed Son steadfastly set his face to go to the city where he was to suffer and die; let there be in us this same devotion which was in him. Forgive us, we beseech thee, our many evasions of duty. We have held back from fear of men. We have ranked security and comfort higher than justice and truth, and our hearts condemn us. But thou, O Lord, who art greater than our hearts, have mercy upon us. Purge us from the fear that is born of self-concern. Beget in us the fear that we may be found wanting in loyalty to thee and thy purpose of good for mankind. Fill us with the compassion of him who for our sake endured the cross; that we may be delivered from selfishness and cowardice; and that, dedicating our lives to thy service, we may be used of thee to help one another and to heal the hurt of the world; through the same Jesus Christ our Lord.[26] Amen.

ERNEST FREMONT TITTLE

About the Lesson

In the book, *The Scarlet Letter,* a man named Arthur Dimsdale tried every possible way to secure forgiveness for his screaming sin and to receive inner peace. He appealed to the town council for clearance of his record but received no freedom from a sense of guilt. He tried disciplined and diligent personal service, only to discover that this too availed nothing. Only when he brought his sin in penitence and confession to the Cross did he find pardon, release, and freedom.

The writer to the Hebrews is reciting somewhat the same kind of biography. The sacrifices of animals were powerless to purify a man, since the sin remained, and the individual himself continued to be an unforgiven sinner. The only effective sacrifice is that made by Christ himself. In support of this conviction the Fortieth Psalm is quoted, "I delight to do thy will, O my God."[a]

The lives of men are disobedient, selfish, often rebellious, so that any man-made sacrifice cannot avail. Jesus is the perfect sacrifice, for he did God's will. He did for us what no one has ever been able to do for himself: he made the perfect complete sacrifice of himself in obedience to divine will. What we could not do, Christ has done, and the way of forgiveness, pardon and peace is open to all.

Someone has summarized in a single sentence what Christian faith means, "There is a Father in heaven who loves us, a Brother Savior who died for us, a Spirit who helps us to be good, and a Home where we shall all meet at last." What a confession of faith!

The Lord's Prayer

---

[a] Psalm 40:8

Live for that which will outlast you.

The Scripture

So the chief priests and the Pharisees gathered the council, and said, "What are we to do? For this man performs many signs. If we let him go on thus, every one will believe in him, and the Romans will come and destroy both our holy place and our nation." But one of them, Caiaphas, who was high priest that year, said to them, "You know nothing at all; you do not understand that it is expedient for you that one man should die for the people, and that the whole nation should not perish." He did not say this of his own accord, but being high priest that year he prophesied that Jesus should die for the nation and not for the nation only, but to gather into one the children of God who are scattered abroad. So from that day on they took counsel how to put him to death.

Jesus therefore no longer went about openly among the Jews, but went from there to the country near the wilderness, to a town called Ephraim; and there he stayed with the disciples.

John 11: 47-54

The Prayer for the Day

Eternal God, our Father, amidst the confusion in this day, life sometimes seems too much for us. Often we slip from tested highways into disillusionment and despair. Our cherished dreams for peace and goodness which have lured us into high adventure are forgotten. The noble heights of vision for personal achievement and a better world have been unscaled and, at times, even our sight grows dim.

When such moods are upon us, dear Father, we turn with greater thankfulness to thee, where the sense of thy unfailing love is made fresh and vivid. We are grateful for the renewal of our sinking spirits, and we rejoice that here assurance is again made strong in the joy of mercy and forgiveness. We thank thee for trustworthy guidance in the way we should walk and for corrected vision to discern life in proper and wholesome perspective.

Thy love is complete and abiding and we pray that thou wilt help us to use the resources given us to understand others and to minister to their need. Amen.

Harry Emerson Fosdick once said that actors portray fiction as though it were real, and preachers sometimes preach truth as though it were fiction. Caiaphas was a person in the divine drama, who made a statement much more important and significant than he knew. "You know nothing at all; you do not understand that it is expedient for you that one man should die for the people, and that the whole nation should not perish."[a] Here Caiaphas intended to say that it was better that Jesus should die to save the nation than that there should be trouble with the Romans so that the whole nation perished. But what Caiaphas said was true in a greater and grander way than he ever dared dream. How often God speaks his divine will and wisdom through the commonplace occurrence and through ordinary people. A person may be an ambassador of the divine will without knowing it, as was Caiaphas.

Jesus was to give his life not for one nation but for all nations and for all people everywhere. The body of Jesus was to be broken so that the brokenness of mankind might be healed.

In one of the early service books of the Christian church called, *The Teaching of the Twelve Apostles,* dating back to the first or second century, there is this impressive statement, "Even as this bread was scattered upon the mountains, and was brought into one, so let thy church be brought together from the ends of the earth." In the sacrifice and death of one man, Jesus Christ, there is a unity and a hope for all men.

THE LORD'S PRAYER

---

[a] John 11:49b-50

I sought my soul, but my soul I could not see. I sought my God, but my God eluded me. I sought my brother, and found all three.

The Scripture

Therefore, brethren, since we have confidence to enter the sanctuary by the blood of Jesus, by the new and living way which he opened for us through the curtain, that is, through his flesh, and since we have a great priest over the house of God, let us draw near with a true heart in full assurance of faith, with our hearts sprinkled clean from an evil conscience and our bodies washed with pure water. Let us hold fast the confession of our hope without wavering, for he who promised is faithful; and let us consider how to stir up one another to love and good works, not neglecting to meet together, as is the habit of some, but encouraging one another, and all the more as you see the Day drawing near.   Hebrews 10: 19-25

THE PRAYER FOR THE DAY

Lord Jesus, bless all who serve, who have dedicated their lives to the ministry of others — all the teachers of schools who labor so patiently with so little appreciation; all who wait upon the public, the clerks in the stores who have to accept criticism, complaints, bad manners, selfishness at the hands of a thoughtless public. Bless the mailman, the drivers of streetcars and buses who must listen to people who lose their tempers.

Bless every humble soul, who, in these days of stress and strain, preaches sermons without words. In the name of him who called men to be the servants of all. Amen.[27]

PETER MARSHALL

Everyone lives in two worlds: the world of time and place, and the world of the spirit and of eternity. How easy to become involved in the world of earthly living to the neglect of the world of the spirit!

Christian life has two gardens: one where food is grown for the sustenance of the body and the other where the spirit is fed by contemplation and in communion with God by the reading of Holy Scripture and by prayer. Every person needs a secret shrine where he enters into the presence of God.

Christian life needs to express itself, if it is to live. The Creed is the statement of what we believe and becomes a confession of faith and a public witness to others. John writes, "That which we have seen and heard we proclaim also to you, so that you may have fellowship with us; and our fellowship is with the Father and with his Son Jesus Christ."[a]

Another Christian duty is to take thought of others. On my desk there is a motto, "I am third." Christ is first in commitment, others are second in my concern, and I am third. It is easy to let our Christian life drift into selfishness; much harder to lose ourselves into eternity. Temptation is great to seek the cynic's seat and to discourage the enthusiasm of others. A word of praise, thanks, or cheer has kept many a life on its feet. Christ's people are those who lift life rather than lean on it. We do not feel the world owes us a living, but rather know that we owe Christ our lives. Christians are anxious to do all the good they can to all the people they can in all the places they can as long as ever they can.

THE LORD'S PRAYER

---

[a] 1 John 1:3

PALM SUNDAY

Heart of Christ my King! I greet thee;
Gladly goes my heart to meet thee;
To embrace thee now it burneth,
And with eager thirst it yearneth,
   Spirit blest, to talk with thee.
Oh, what love divine compelling!
With what grief thy breast was swelling!
All thy soul for us o'erflowing,
All thy life on us bestowing,
   Sinful men from death to free!

Oh, that death! in bitter anguish,
Cruel, pitiless to languish!
To the inmost cell it entered,
Where the life of man was centered,
   Gnawing thy sweet heartstrings there.
From that death which thou hast tasted,
For that form by sorrow wasted,
Heart to my heart ever nearest,
Kindle in me love the dearest;
   This, O Lord, is all my prayer.

O sweet Heart! My choicest blessing,
Cleanse my heart, its sin confessing;
Hardened in its worldly folly,
Make it soft again, and holy,
   Melting all its icy ground.
To my heart's core come, and quicken
Me a sinner, conscience-stricken;
Be thy grace my soul renewing,
All its power to thee subduing,
   Languishing with love's sweet wound.

To thy holy heart, oh, take me!
Thy companion, Jesu, make me,
In that sorrow joy exceeding,
In that beauty scarred and bleeding,
   Till my heart be wholly thine.
Rest, my soul! now naught shall sever;
After thee it follows ever;
Here its thirst finds glad fulfilling;
Jesu! be thou not unwilling,
   Take this loving heart of mine!

St. Bernard of Clairvaux, 1091-1153
Tr. E. A. Washburn of New York, 1868

RECEIVE THE LOVE OF HIS HEART

The Scripture

> Now as they were eating, Jesus took bread, and blessed, and broke it, and gave it to the disciples and said, "Take, eat; this is my body." And he took a cup, and when he had given thanks he gave it to them, saying, "Drink of it, all of you; for this is my blood of the covenant, which is poured out for many for the forgiveness of sins." Matthew 26: 26-28

The hymns in this book, introducing the sermons for the Sundays in Lent, are ascribed by tradition to St. Bernard of Clairvaux, who lived in the twelfth century. The Latin original is found in the poem "Rhythmica Oratio," which was composed of seven distinct parts. These sections portray the worshiper at the foot of the cross, directing his words to the broken body of the dying Lord. Paul Gerhardt translated the hymns into a gripping German version, which has become a veritable classical hymn series, often assigned to German confirmation classes for memorization. Several translations from the German have been made into English. It is interesting to read a notation on the original Latin script, which reads, "As now St. Bernard had spoken these words with quiet earnestness of desire, the image on the cross bowed itself and embraced him with its wounded arms, as a sure token that to it this prayer was most pleasing."

To ponder and meditate upon the broken body of the Lord does excite an experience of response, not on the Master's part, for that has already been given, but on our part in worshiping and addressing him, as our Lord and Savior and Sovereign. It is this priceless joy of thanksgiving, confession and adoration that becomes ours in the Sacrament of the Altar.

Undoubtedly you are familiar with the experience of many who have visited the Cathedral in Copenhagen to see Thorwaldson's masterpiece, "Kommer till mig." The guide invites all who wish to see it fully to kneel at the altar and to look up into the Master's tilted face. It is in the posture of prayer that the masterwork is comprehended best. It is on our knees that we begin to understand the meaning of the Master's words, "This is my body broken," and "This is my blood shed for the forgiveness of sins."

Divine intimacy of the heart is communicated in several ways. We might never know of anyone's love unless it were expressed in words. If God is to reveal himself to us in a heart-to-heart relationship, then he must tell his love by speaking to us. And God has spoken. His holy words are written for us to hear, "I have loved you with an everlasting love."[a] Beyond speech love must express itself in action. And so God became incarnate in Jesus Christ, living in human and humble form, forgiving sin and giving peace. God's love is in action in Jesus Christ, revealing that we are unworthy to live, but that he loves us so that we can live to be worthy. But this heart-to-heart relationship not only speaks and acts, it also gives. In the Sacrament of the Altar, Jesus gives himself to all, with his body broken and his blood shed for our redemption. We receive the love of his heart in Holy Communion.

The Sacrament of the Altar is a personal giving of the Lord himself to his own for the remission of sins. It is God's call to us, "Return to the Lord, your God, for he is gracious and merciful, slow to anger, and abounding in steadfast love, and repents of evil."[b] Here is God's life for his people, in the fullness of his loving heart.

No one can completely and adequately define and describe the Holy Sacrament. To put its full significance into words would be like trying to wrap up an article too large with a piece of paper that is too small. We cannot enclose a big picture with a little frame. When everything has been said about the meaning of the Lord's Supper that can be said, all

---

[a] Jer. 31:3
[b] Joel 2:13

has not been said, for it is beyond the understanding of mortal man. It is of God!

Our reason cannot tell us what the Lord's Supper is, nor our sense of taste or touch, but only the Word of God. Concerning the bread in this Sacrament, the Word of God speaks as follows: "Take, eat; this is my body."[c] "Take, this is my body."[d] "This is my body."[e] Concerning the wine, we read: "Drink of it, all of you; for this is my blood of the covenant, which is poured out for many for the forgiveness of sins."[f] "This is my blood of the covenant, which is poured out for many."[g] "This cup is the new covenant in my blood."[h]

The Sacrament of the Altar is the Lord's Table, upon which God gives us his abundant undeserved love in Christ Jesus. This feast of the Lord's refreshes and satisfies us, increases our faith, and helps us grow in godliness. Mephiboseth declined the king's invitation because he was crippled, until the king reminded him that when seated at his feast, the table would cover his infirmity.[i] The Lord's Supper is such a table, covering and forgiving our iniquities and trespasses.

Oftentimes the Sacrament of the Altar is called "Eucharist," which means "thanksgiving." As we kneel at the altar to receive the Sacrament we are publicly acknowledging our irreparable and everlasting indebtedness to him, whose we are, whom we serve, and to whom we go. "Bless the Lord, O my soul; and all that is within me, bless his holy name! Bless the Lord, O my soul, and forget not all his benefits, who forgives all your iniquity."[j]

The Lord's Supper is the testament or covenant of Christ,

---

[c] Matt. 26:26
[d] Mark 14:22
[e] Luke 22:19
[f] Matt. 26:27-28
[g] Mark 14:24
[h] 1 Cor. 11:25
[i] 2 Samuel 9
[j] Psalm 103:1-3

for he says, "This cup is the new covenant in my blood."[k] A covenant or will is a gift. In the Lord's Supper, it is God, who in Christ, stoops down to us and gives us himself. "Thanks be to God for his inexpressible gift!"[l] It is this gift which grants eternal life to all who, in faith, receive it.

It is a fellowship. It is a unity of joy and blessing with other believers in the crucified Savior. Across continents, cultures, and "colors" the Sacrament makes of all Christian believers one body, for it is the bond of the whole Christian family on earth and in heaven too! Many of those communing may be strangers to us by personal acquaintance, but they are friends to us by faith. Alice Meynell wrote long ago:

> One of the crowd went up,
> And knelt before the Paten and the Cup,
> Received the Lord, returned in peace,
>   and prayed
> Close to my side. Then in my heart
> I said:
> "O Christ, in this man's life —
> This stranger who is thine . . ."[28]

We commune at one altar, in one fellowship, because of one Christ who gives us again and anew his redemption through the Holy Sacrament. When a pastor confirms his own child, he perhaps understands as none other that the bond of faith is stronger than the bond of blood.

In the Lord's Supper we receive forgiveness for sins, freedom from evil and eternal. These are gifts infinitely more precious than gold or costly jewels, for here we receive the very life of God. It is not work that wears us out; it is worries and sins that make us weary. But in the Lord's Supper we receive peace through the forgiveness of sins and release from our worries as the Lord lifts our burdens from our spirits and strengthens our souls with the resources of his power.

---

[k] 1 Cor. 11:25
[l] 2 Cor. 9:15

118

"Sweet the moments, rich in blessing,
Which before the Cross we spend,
Life and health and peace possessing
From the sinner's dying Friend."

The Sacrament of the Altar is a mystery. This Communion of our life with him, who is the Life of Life, is in its essence beyond our knowing. It is something which we can never fully penetrate with our deepest thought, for here our "life is hid with Christ in God."[m] For it is incomprehensible that in this world of sin and death, God has introduced him, who is the King of life, and has called us to be one with him and to share his life.

Holy Communion is a privilege that we cannot buy, for there is not enough money in the wide world to purchase it. It is a gift which we cannot earn, for there is not toil enough to merit it. It is a gift, which our thinking cannot fully appropriate, for its divine wisdom is above us. But, wonders of wonders, it is given freely and abundantly to all who believe.

And we are worthy to receive it when we know ourselves to be unworthy. It is given to those who know themselves to be sinners and not perfect saints. It is meant for those who confess their sins and who hunger and thirst after righteousness. "Whoever, therefore, eats the bread or drinks the cup of the Lord in an unworthy manner will be guilty of profaning the body and blood of the Lord. Let a man examine himself, and so eat of the bread and drink of the cup."[n]

To any and to all Christ invites in these words, "And him who comes to me I will not cast out."[o] Again Jesus says, "If any one thirst, let him come to me and drink."[p] To those who long for forgiveness and for power to live in the fullness of the joy of God — come!

---

[m] Colossians 3:3
[n] 1 Cor. 11:27-28
[o] John 6:37
[p] John 7:37

119

We come, not because we must, but because we may; not because we are strong, but because we are weak; not because we claim heaven's rewards, but because in our frailty and sin we need heaven's mercy. And so we come.

How gratefully and gladly we accept the love of his heart!

We never knew we were asleep until we awakened; and we never knew what sin was until it had been forgiven.

The Scripture

And as they led him away, they seized one Simon of Cyrene, who was coming in from the country, and laid on him the cross, to carry it behind Jesus. And there followed him a great multitude of the people, and of women who bewailed and lamented him. But Jesus turning to them said, "Daughters of Jerusalem, do not weep for me, but weep for yourselves and for your children. For behold, the days are coming when they will say, 'Blessed are the barren, and the wombs that never bore, and the breasts that never gave suck!' Then they will begin to say to the mountains, 'Fall on us'; and to the hills 'Cover us.' For if they do this when the wood is green, what will happen when it is dry?"

Two others also, who were criminals, were led away to be put to death with him. And when they came to the place which is called The Skull, there they crucified him, and the criminals, one on the right and one on the left. And Jesus said, "Father, forgive them; for they know not what they do." And they cast lots to divide his garments. And the people stood by, watching; but the rulers scoffed at him, saying, "He saved others; let him save himself, if he is the Christ of God, his Chosen One!" The soldiers also mocked him, coming up and offering him vinegar, and saying, "If you are the King of the Jews, save yourself!" There was also an inscription over him, "This is the King of the Jews."   Luke 23: 26-38

THE PRAYER FOR THE DAY

O Lord Jesus Christ, Prince of Peace, who, when thou wast reviled, didst not revile again, and who on the cross didst pray for those who nailed thee there: Implant in our hearts the virtues of gentleness and patience, that we may overcome evil with good, for thy sake love our enemies, and as children of our heavenly Father seek thy peace, and evermore rejoice in thy love. Amen.[29]

Our Lord spoke seven times from the cross, and these are called "His Seven Last Words." In the Sacrament of the Altar we receive bread, which is crushed grain: and wine, which is crushed fruit. From the cross during the saying of His seven last words, we are listening to the outcries of the crushed body of Christ.

The Lord, during his earthly life, used many varied and strange pulpits from which to preach the words of life. Sometimes his pulpit was a boat on the sea, the gate of the Temple, or Jacob's well. He spoke his valedictory from the pulpit of the cross, which makes these words remembered down the arches of the years. Here he offered himself! With heavy hammer-blows, he was fastened to the cross. And the cross was lifted slowly off the ground and with a sharp thud, that seemed to shake even hell, dropped into the pit prepared for it. The Lord mounted his last pulpit. From the cross came an eloquent sermon.

His first word from the cross is "Father, forgive them; for they know not what they do."[a] In the crucifixion a tree turns against the Master, and becomes a cross. Iron turns against him, and becomes nails. Roses turn against him, and become thorns. Men turn against him, and become executioners. He speaks a prayer for all, "Father, forgive them; for they know not what they do." Jesus, dying, needed no forgiveness, for he had no sin. But he requested forgiving grace for those who crucified him, knowing how much our human lives need the grace of God. Forgiveness is not cheap. If it were offered without a Cross, who would accept its worth? But from a scarred broken body, who can refuse? The Cross is the price God paid to buy us from our sins.

THE LORD'S PRAYER

---

[a] Luke 23:34

Real life is relationship with God! Separation from him is hell; salvation in him is heaven.

The Scripture

One of the criminals who was hanged railed at him, saying, "Are you not the Christ? Save yourself and us!" But the other rebuked him, saying, "Do you not fear God, since you are under the same sentence of condemnation? And we indeed justly; for we are receiving the due reward of our deeds; but this man has done nothing wrong." And he said, "Jesus, remember me when you come in your kingly power." And he said to him, "Truly, I say to you, today you will be with me in Paradise." Luke 23: 39-43

THE PRAYER FOR THE DAY

O Holy Jesus, who, of thine infinite mercy, didst accept the conversion of a sinner upon the cross: Open thine eyes of mercy, we beseech thee, upon all those who know thy love yet delay giving thee their allegiance and devotion; and of thy pity hasten the day when all men, drawn to thee by thy cross, shall call thee Lord and Master and rejoice in life dedicated to thee. Amen.[30]

The second word from the cross is spoken by the Redeemer hanging between the unredeemed, for the Scripture says, "Two others also, who were criminals, were led away to be put to death with him."[a] At the beginning of the crucifixion they both cursed the Savior, but suddenly one turned to the central cross and requested to be one of his subjects, saying, "Jesus, remember me when you come in your kingly power."[b] The thief addressed the central cross by name, "Jesus," indicating that he knew who it was with whom he was crucified; he had no reservations about speaking to Jesus directly. The criminal's prayer, "Remember me," had something of pathos about it, for how could the crucified Christ ever forget anyone? And the prayer concludes, "when you come in your kingly power." How could the criminal understand that the central cross belonged to a king, who had power? Did the crown of thorns indicate his kingship, or did the thief sense that this crucifixion on the central cross was really a coronation?

Since no prayer to God ever is unanswered, there comes a quick reply. From the crucified Christ come these words, "Today you shall be with me in Paradise." "Today" means that while evil may have its hour, God will have his day. The word "you" reminds us that any person, even an outcast, is of such infinite worth that Christ addresses him with respect. And the words, "shall be with me in Paradise.", reveal the wonder of grace that it does not take much time to redeem; it only takes much love.

THE LORD'S PRAYER

---

[a] Luke 23:32
[b] Luke 23:42

Men return to God not because they are good, but because they know they need him.

The Scripture

So they took Jesus, and he went out, bearing his own cross, to the place called the place of a skull, which is called in Hebrew Golgotha. There they crucified him, and with him two others, one on either side, and Jesus between them. Pilate also wrote a title and put it on the cross; it read, "Jesus of Nazareth, the King of the Jews." Many of the Jews read this title, for the place where Jesus was crucified was near the city; and it was written in Hebrew, in Latin, and in Greek. The chief priests of the Jews then said to Pilate, "Do not write, 'The king of the Jews,' but, 'This man said, I am King of the Jews.'" Pilate answered, "What I have written I have written."

When the soldiers had crucified Jesus they took his garments and made four parts, one for each soldier. But his tunic was without seam, woven from top to bottom; so they said to one another, "Let us not tear it, but cast lots for it to see whose it shall be." This was to fulfill the scripture "They parted my garments among them, and for my clothing they cast lots."

So the soldiers did this, but standing by the cross of Jesus were his mother, and his mother's sister, Mary, the wife of Clopas, and Mary Magdalene. When Jesus saw his mother, and the disciple whom he loved standing near, he said to his mother, "Woman, behold your son!" Then he said to the disciple, "Behold your mother!" And from that hour the disciple took her to his own home.   John 19: 17-27

THE PRAYER FOR THE DAY

O Lord Jesus, who while thou didst suffer the agony of the Cross didst show thy love for thy sorrowing Mother: We implore thee, regard in tender pity all parents whose hearts are torn by the loss of loved ones or heavily laden with worries over self-willed and strayed children; and, of thy mercy, gather all within the peace of thy Cross, so that the bond of parenthood and childhood may be welded in love of thee. Amen.[31]

In the third word from the cross, Jesus addressed himself to the two most intimate friends he had on earth, his mother, Mary, and the disciple whom Jesus loved, John, and to them he said, "Woman, behold your son!" Then he said to the disciple, "Behold your mother!"[a] He spoke to them as "woman" and "son," trying to help them see that faith and trust in God were personal relationships as wide as the world. He was teaching them that there were more important ties than those of flesh and blood. There were bonds of faith involving the whole family of God on earth. "Here are my mother and my brothers! Whoever does the will of God is my brother, and sister, and mother."[b]

Christianity is never an individual affair. Christianity always involves relationships. Jesus tried to teach Mary and John the grace of sharing responsibilities. Our Lord died for all men and not only for those who were close to him. So long as each individual tries to exist for himself, there is social maladjustment and discontent. Whenever any person or any class or any nation seeks its own interests exclusively, there are difficulties. The equal distribution of goods and aid does not make men brothers, but when all men know the Father through Christ, then economic aid is distributed. The prodigal son thought he could have peace when he had received his share of the family wealth, but he had none until he re-established a right relationship with his father. Live for others, and you will begin to live for yourself.

The third word from the cross is a remedy for selfishness and asks us to begin acknowledging our associations with all others as sons of God and brothers of Christ.

THE LORD'S PRAYER

---

[a] John 19:26-27
[b] Mark 3:34-35

If we think that we know it all, how can God teach us what we do not know?

The Scripture

And those who passed by derided him, wagging their heads and saying, "You who would destroy the temple and build it in three days, save yourself! If you are the Son of God, come down from the cross." So also the chief priests, with the scribes and elders, mocked him, saying, "He saved others; he cannot save himself. He is the King of Israel; let him come down now from the cross, and we will believe in him. He trusts in God; let God deliver him now, if he desires him; for he said, 'I am the Son of God.'" And the robbers who were crucified with him also reviled him in the same way.

Now from the sixth hour there was darkness over all the land until the ninth hour. And about the ninth hour Jesus cried with a loud voice, Eli, Eli, lama sabachthani?" that is "My God, my God, why hast thou forsaken me?" And some of the bystanders hearing it said, "This man is calling Elijah."

Matthew 27: 39-47

THE PRAYER FOR THE DAY

O God, Almighty Creator of heaven and earth, who holdest in thine hand all the might of man: Forsake not thy world which thy Son hath redeemed by his holy Cross, but which is sore beset by the power of sin and the evils of man; that righteousness may be the health of every nation and the glory of Christ's salvation may be the sure possession of every heart. Amen.[32]

The fourth word from the Cross is as old as man and as new as this moment's perplexity: "My God, why . . . ?" For almost three hours the Lord had hung upon the cross; even the sun began to wear darkness in mourning for him, who is the light of life. Men could look on the Crucifixion, but the sun could not endure it and hid its face. The fourth word, "My God, my God, why hast thou forsaken me?" is an echo of the Twenty-second Psalm. During his life some of his disciples had left him; one betrayed him, and now even God seemed to abandon him.

Christ in this word experiences abandonment. No one can know the deeper meaning of this cry. At the moment Jesus permitted himself to feel the solitariness and abandonment caused by all the sin of the world and life's mysterious ways, and yet this cry indicates that even in abandonment God cannot be forgotten, for the word is prefaced by "My God, my God."

When Adam had sinned, he hid himself, and God asked, "Where are you?"[a] Now the new Adam understands loneliness of heart and asks God, "Where are you?" How strangely haunting, yet reassuring, is the realization that even when we imagine it, God never ever abandons us, even though we may abandon him.

The fourth word teaches us that the object of faith is God. When Christ was crucified, darkness covered the earth, even as darkness comes today into life when the Light of the World is forgotten. We can trust God even when it seems our lives in the agonies of unwanted experiences are abandoned by him.

THE LORD'S PRAYER

---

[a] Gen. 3:9

L.

Beneath the ashes of sinful lives there are to be found sparks, which can be fanned into flame.

The Scripture

> **After this Jesus, knowing that all was now finished, said (to fulfill the scripture), "I thirst." A bowl full of vinegar stood there; so they put a sponge full of the vinegar on hyssop and held it to his mouth.** John 19: 28-29

THE PRAYER FOR THE DAY

O Lord and Savior, who didst endure the Cross for our sakes, and in bitterest suffering of flesh and spirit didst atone for our sins: We thirst for thy healing strength, and beseech thee, be present with us in all hours of pain and anguish, ever bringing to our remembrance this all which thou hast borne for us; and strengthen us to carry our burdens and to endure our sufferings by the grace of thy holy example, always giving thee thanks for thy love. Amen.[33]

It is often reported that no pain in life is comparable to the anguish borne of thirst. After three hours on the cross, bareheaded under the burning, blinding sun, with his wounds tearing away at his body, the cry comes from the cross, "I thirst." Strange to hear these words from Jesus, who had said, "He who believes in me shall never thirst."[a] and again, he said, "If anyone thirst, let him come to me and drink."[b] Now Jesus turns to men and says, "I thirst." This was spoken "to fulfill the scripture" as given by the psalmist, "They gave me poison for food, and for my thirst they gave me vinegar to drink."[c]

But the thirst on the part of Christ was really for the souls of men, as He sought to fulfill his mission of bringing redemption to all. "And I have other sheep, that are not of this fold; I must bring them also, and they will heed my voice. So there shall be one flock, one shepherd."[d] This fifth word is another manner of invitation, "Come unto me."

The request was not addressed to anyone in particular; but a soldier heard it and ran to answer the need. The vinegar-filled sponge was not much of a gift, but the worth of service is not dependent on the size of the gift but rather on the spirit and intention of the giver. The torch of faith has been handed each of us not to keep, but to use to kindle the flame of faith for other men. In the need of the broken world for physical relief and for evangelization, we can hear the modern cry from the cross, "I thirst." The greatest thirst of all is the thirst of grace unreceived, like the hand reached out which is never clasped or the arm outstretched, which is never embraced, or the hand knocking on a door, which is never opened.

THE LORD'S PRAYER

---

[a] John 6:35
[b] John 7:37
[c] Psalm 69:21
[d] John 10:16

SATURDAY IN HOLY WEEK

Unless there is a Good Friday in our lives, there will never be an Easter, for unless we lose our lives, we shall not find them, unless we are crucified with Christ, we shall never rise with him.

The Scripture

When Jesus had received the vinegar, he said, "It is finished"; and he bowed his head and gave up his spirit.   John 19:30

It was now about the sixth hour, and there was darkness over the whole land until the ninth hour, while the sun's light failed; and the curtain of the temple was torn in two. Then Jesus, crying with a loud voice, said, "Father, into thy hands I commit my spirit!" And having said this he breathed his last. Now when the centurion saw what had taken place, he praised God, and said, "Certainly this man was innocent!" And all the multitudes who assembled to see the sight, when they saw what had taken place, returned home, beating their breasts. And all his acquaintances and the women who had followed him from Galilee stood at a distance and saw these things.

Luke 23: 44-49

THE PRAYER FOR THE DAY

O Lord Jesus Christ, who ever livest to make intercession for us, who hast taken the sting from death and robbed the grave of its victory; to whom is given the name which is above every name, for thou art Lord of all: We implore thee, that, washed of our sin in thy blood, and made children of God through thy victory, and ever strengthened by thy grace, we may be thine through all our days and in the hour of our death; so that by thy mercy we may taste the fruition of thy glorious triumph and come to the peace and joy which thou hast prepared for those who love thee, who with the Father and the Holy Ghost, livest and reignest, God, blessed now and evermore. Amen.[34]

Three times the phrase "It is finished" appears in Scripture: at the time of creation at the conclusion of John's prophecy in Revelation, and in the very center of Holy Scripture. This is the Genesis statement, "Thus the heavens and the earth were finished."[a] And from the Book of Revelation we read, "And a great voice came out of the temple, from the throne, saying, 'It is done.'"[b] Between the alpha and omega is the sixth word, "It is finished."

Jesus makes his report to the heavenly Father as though he were saying, "You have given mankind into my hands for a time, and now my task has been accomplished, for redemption and salvation are completed." The real battle in life is over, and truth is demonstrated as more powerful than falsehood: giving more significant than getting; and sharing more meaningful than saving. The power of sin and evil is broken and victory is accomplished.

With this conclusion to his mission, Jesus speaks his valedictory, "Father, into thy hands I commit my spirit." Greek philosophy announced that the perfect movement of life was the circular one, because the beginning was the end and the end was the beginning. So it was with the life of Jesus, coming from God and now returning to God, he had completed his life's orbit. Prodigal-like for thirty-three years, he had been "wasting his substance," giving his life away, and now he returned home to his Father's house. He spoke in a loud clear voice, for men did not take his life away; he was laying it down. Having had grace to live, he now has grace to die. "Father, into thy hands I commit my spirit."

THE LORD'S PRAYER

---

[a] Gen. 2:1
[b] Rev. 16:17

Now all is still
Time holds his breath upon the hill.
No word is said.
The Lord of heaven and earth is dead.

Under the wood, I'll kneel in grief and gratitude.
I can but kneel.
There are no words for what I feel.

Fold, my hands, fold.
Beat, oh my heart, a prayer untold
Tears, have your way.
My Lord is dead.
I live for aye.[35]

Now after the sabbath, toward the dawn of the first day of the week, Mary Magdalene and the other Mary went to see the sepulchre. And behold, there was a great earthquake; for an angel of the Lord descended from heaven and came and rolled back the stone, and sat upon it. His appearance was like lightning, and his raiment white as snow. And for fear of him the guards trembled and became like dead men. But the angel said to the women, "Do not be afraid; for I know that you seek Jesus who was crucified. He is not here; for he has risen, as he said. Come, see the place where he lay. Then go quickly and tell his disciples that he has risen from the dead, and behold, he is going before you to Galilee; there you will see him. Lo, I have told you."

Matthew 28: 1-7

Acknowledgements

Grateful acknowledgment is made to authors and publishers, who have permitted their materials to be used in this book. Every effort has been made to respect copyrights. If, in any instance, such acknowledgment has been inadvertently omitted, I hope that I may be informed of the oversight so that proper credit may be given in future editions. Grateful acknowledgment is made to Ruth Tubbesing, my most excellent and efficient secretary, for typing and checking the manuscript. Most of all, I am grateful to my dear life partner, Ruth Person Hammarberg, for inspiration, encouragement, and affection, as well as to my children, Melvyn, Linda, Jon, and Paul, who believe this writing may have merit. The following have granted permission for the reprinting of copyrighted materials from books and periodicals:

[1]From *The Meaning and Message of Lent* by Eugene R. Fairweather. Publishers, Harper & Row, Publishers, Incorporated, New York.

[2]Prayer from Collects and Prayers for Use in Church, authorized by The United Lutheran Church in America, Philadelphia, Pennsylvania.

[3]Prayer from *Minister's Service Book,* compiled and edited by James Dalton Morrison. Publishers, Harper & Row, Publishers, Incorporated, New York.

[4]From *Modern Man in Search of a Soul* by Carl G. Jung. Publishers, Harcourt, Brace & World, Inc., New York.

[5]Poem, "The Man Christ" by Therese Lindsey.

[6]Author of this poem is E. S. Martin (1856-1939).

[7]Prayer by Joseph Fort Newton in *Altar Stairs* by Jennie Mai Newton. Harry J. J. Bellwoar, Jr., Attorney for the Estate of Jennie Mai Newton, Dec'd., Philadelphia, Pennsylvania.

[8]Reprinted from *Look*, April 24, 1962, issue. Copyright 1962 by Cowles Magazines & Broadcasting, Inc., New York.

[9]Prayer by Bishop Ken from *Prayers for the City of God* by Gilbert Clive Binyon. Publishers, Longmans, Green & Co. Limited, London, England.

136

[10]Prayer by Walter Rauschenbusch in *Prayers of the Social Awakening*. The Pilgrim Press, Boston, Massachusetts.

[11]Prayer by Ashton Oxenden from *Prayers for Living* compiled by Hazel T. Wilson.

[12]Prayer by Simon Patrick from *Prayers for Living* compiled by Hazel T. Wilson.

[13]Paraphrases of an anecdote from *Lord of All Life* by A. Ian Burnett, published by Clarke, Irwin & Company Limited, Toronto, Canada.

[14]Poem, "His Hands" by John Richard Moreland, from *Masterpieces of Religious Verse*. By permission of Harper & Brothers.

[15]Prayer in *The Eternal Voice* by The Rev. Dr. Leslie D. Weatherhead, C.B.E., Sussex, England.

[16]Prayer by Charles Wolcott Merriam from *Prayers for Living* compiled by Hazel T. Wilson. Copyright 1955 by Pierce and Washabaugh. By permission of Abingdon Press.

[17]From the "Hound of Heaven" by Francis Thompson. By permission of Burns, Oates & Washbourne, Ltd., London, England.

[18]From "The Road Not Taken" from *Complete Poems by Robert Frost*. Copyright 1916, 1921 by Holt, Rinehart and Winston, Inc. Copyright renewed 1944 by Robert Frost. Reprinted by permission of Holt, Rinehart and Winston, Inc.

[19]Excerpt from "The Burden of the Christian" by Charles Malik, from December 20, 1961 issue. Copyright 1961 Christian Century Foundation. Reprinted by permission from *The Christian Century*.

[20]From *Sunday Evening Sermons* by Alton M. Motter. By permission of Harper & Brothers, New York.

[21]From *Minister's Service Book*, compiled and edited by James Dalton Morrison. By permission of Harper & Brothers, New York.

[22]Prayer from *A Book of Pastoral Prayers* by Ernest Fremont Tittle. Copyright c 1951 by Pierce and Smith. By permission of Abingdon Press.

[23]By Helen Howarth Lemmel, published in *Youth's Favorite Songs* by Augustana Luther League, Minneapolis, Minnesota.

[24]Illustration by Dr. George A. Buttrick, Wilmette, Illinois.

[25]Poem by John Oxenham from *Bees in Amber*, published by the American Tract Society, New York.

[26]Prayer from *A Book of Pastoral Prayers* by Ernest Fremont Tittle. Copyright c 1951 by Pierce and Smith. By permission of Abingdon Press.

[27]Prayer, "For Those Who Serve" by Peter Marshall from *The Prayers of Peter Marshall*. By permission of McGraw-Hill Book Company, Inc., New York, publisher.

[28]Poem by Alice Meynell from *The Poems of Alice Meynell*. By permission of Burns, Oates & Washbourne, Ltd., London, England.

[29]through [34]Prayers in the book, *Collects and Prayers* for Use in Church, authorized by The United Lutheran Church in America, Philadelphia.

[35]Poem, "Now All Is Still." Author unknown.

[31]From *Prayers For Today* by Samuel McComb. Copyright 1918 by Harper and Brothers. (Refers to footnote on page 20.)

Date Due

138

Code 4386-04, CLS-4, Broadman Supplies, Nashville, Tenn., Printed in U.S.A.